GRADE
8

P9-CNI-741

CORE SKILLS

Language Arts

ISBN 0-7398-7095-5

11 12 13 0982 12 11 10

Steck Vaughn™

A Harcourt Achieve Imprint

www.Steck-Vaughn.com
1-800-531-5015

Contents

Introduction

Core Skills: Language Arts was developed to help your child improve the language skills he or she needs to succeed. The book emphasizes skills in the key areas of

- grammar
- punctuation
- vocabulary
- writing
- research

The more than 100 lessons included in the book provide many opportunities for your child to practice and apply important language and writing skills. These skills will help your child excel in all academic areas, increase his or her scores on standardized tests, and have a greater opportunity for success in his or her career.

About the Book

The book is divided into six units:

- Parts of Speech
- Sentences
- Mechanics
- Vocabulary and Usage
- Writing
- Research Skills

Your child can work through each unit of the book, or you can pinpoint areas that need extra practice.

Lessons have specific instructions and examples and are designed for your child to complete independently. Grammar lessons range from using nouns and verbs to constructing better sentences. Writing exercises range from the personal narrative to the research report. With this practice, your child will gain extra confidence as he or she works on daily school lessons or standardized tests.

A thorough answer key is also provided to check the quality of answers.

A Step Toward Success

Practice may not always make perfect, but it is certainly a step in the right direction. The activities in *Core Skills: Language Arts* are an excellent way to ensure greater success for your child.

Kinds of Nouns

A **noun** names a person, place, thing, or idea.
Examples:
  teacher, school, book, anger
A **common noun** names any person, place, thing, or idea. It begins with a lowercase letter.
Examples:
  writer, park, poem, joy
A **proper noun** names a particular person, place, thing, or idea. Each important word in a proper noun begins with a capital letter.
Examples:
  Oprah Winfrey, Chicago, Declaration of Independence, Federalism
A **concrete noun** names things that you can see and touch.
Examples:
  pizza, kitten, diamond, telephone
An **abstract noun** names an idea, quality, action, or feeling.
Examples:
  opinion, beauty, happiness
A **collective noun** names a group of persons or things.
Examples:
  crowd, flock, family

DIRECTIONS ➤ Read each sentence. Add the kind of noun named in parentheses.

1. All the (collective noun) applauded when (proper noun) appeared on (common noun).

2. (proper noun) is fascinating because it has (concrete noun).

3. The students like (proper noun) because she shows concern for everyone.

4. Some (common noun) could do a better job if they had more (abstract noun).

5. (proper noun) shows (abstract noun) to all the (common noun).

6. (proper noun) likes the (common noun) because of all its (abstract noun).

7. Unfortunately, these (concrete noun) do not display enough (abstract noun).

8. (proper noun) should have used the (common noun) to develop more (abstract noun).

9. The (collective noun) of cattle stampeded across the (common noun).

10. Your (abstract noun) has helped many (collective noun) buy (concrete noun).

Singular and Plural Nouns

> A **singular noun** names one person, place, thing, or idea.
> *Examples:*
> > musician, office, bracelet, courage
> A **plural noun** names more than one person, place, thing, or idea.
> *Examples:*
> > musicians, offices, bracelets

DIRECTIONS ▷ **The underlined nouns in these sentences should be plural. Write each sentence using the correct plural forms.**

1. After the concert, all the <u>alto</u> went out for <u>taco</u>.

   _____

2. There were three <u>patio</u>, but the <u>singer</u> couldn't decide where to sit.

   _____

   _____

3. Some sat beneath the overhanging <u>branch</u> of <u>tree</u>; <u>other</u> sat near the <u>bush</u>.

   _____

   _____

4. The waiter brought them <u>fork</u>, <u>spoon</u>, and <u>knife</u>.

   _____

5. Then he asked if the women wanted <u>tomato</u> and <u>avocado</u> with their <u>taco</u>.

   _____

   _____

6. Crab <u>salad</u> were served in <u>half</u> of <u>cantaloupe</u>.

   _____

7. "We should all come back with our <u>family</u>," said one woman.

   _____

8. Most <u>Saturday</u>, Margaret watches the <u>orchestra</u> play <u>symphony</u>.

   _____

9. The <u>costume</u> of the <u>actor</u> are very colorful and attractive.

   _____

10. The <u>musician</u> play <u>guitar</u>, <u>accordion</u>, and <u>violin</u>.

   _____

Irregular Plural Nouns

To form some **plural nouns**, add or change letters.
Examples:
>   foot, feet   child, children

For some plural nouns, the plural is the same as the singular form.
Examples:
>   sheep, sheep   scissors, scissors

If you don't know the correct plural of a noun, look up the word in a dictionary. Plural forms are shown immediately after the main entry words.

DIRECTIONS → Write the singular or plural form of each noun as indicated.

1. one trout, two _____
2. one deer, two _____
3. one ox, two _____
4. two sheep, one _____
5. one shellfish, two _____
6. one waltz, two _____
7. one father-in-law, two _____
8. one species, two _____
9. one capful, two _____
10. one hero, two _____

11. two alumni, one _____
12. one calf, two _____
13. two passersby, one _____
14. one tooth, two _____
15. two aspirin, one _____
16. two mice, one _____
17. two women, one _____
18. one attorney-at-law, two _____
19. two dice, one _____
20. two men, one _____

DIRECTIONS → The underlined nouns in these sentences should be plural. Write each sentence using the correct plural forms.

21. When the <u>fox</u> entered the barnyard, all the <u>goose</u>, <u>chicken</u>, and <u>sheep</u> panicked.

_____

22. Before the <u>child</u> put an end to the turmoil, several <u>crate</u> of <u>zucchini</u> had been trampled.

_____

23. My <u>friend</u> gave me three <u>scarf</u> for my birthday.

_____

24. The <u>editor-in-chief</u> wrote the article about the computer <u>glitch</u>.

_____

25. The <u>man</u> carrying the <u>umbrella</u> had <u>box</u> of <u>blueberry</u>.

_____

Possessive Nouns

A **possessive noun** shows ownership.
Example:
> the acting career of my friend   my *friend's* acting career

Add an apostrophe **(')**, and *s* to form the possessive of singular nouns.
Examples:
> person's, artist's, teacher's

Add an apostrophe to form the possessive of most plural nouns ending in *s*.
Examples:
> persons', artists', teachers'

If a plural noun does not end in *s*, add an apostrophe and *s* to form the possessive.
Examples:
> mice's, women's, trout's

DIRECTIONS ▷ Rewrite the following as possessives, using the apostrophe correctly.

1. the music of a teenager _____
2. the music of teenagers _____
3. the dog of my neighbor _____
4. the yard of my neighbors _____
5. the dashboard in the car _____
6. the erasers on the pencils _____
7. the pool belonging to Molly _____
8. the history of Texas _____
9. the bikes of the brothers _____
10. the fish belonging to Agnes _____
11. the street where my stepsister lives _____
12. the two cats of Amanda Jones _____
13. the eyes of the students _____
14. the contribution made by Bess _____
15. the testimony of a witness _____
16. the ideas of children _____
17. the classroom of the eighth-graders _____
18. the hats worn by construction workers _____
19. the cabin owned by the Bodettes _____
20. doghouse of Rex _____
21. the tusks of the elephants _____
22. the ending of the story _____

Personal Pronouns

A **personal pronoun** takes the place of a noun or nouns.
Examples:

Bill McCoy heard.   *He* heard.   The *boys* heard.   *They* heard.

Personal pronouns show number and gender. Number tells whether a pronoun is singular or plural. Gender tells whether a pronoun is masculine, feminine, or neuter.
Examples:

Singular
I, me, my, mine
you, your, yours
he, him, his
she, her, hers
it, its

Plural
we, us, our, ours
you, your, yours
they, them, their, theirs

DIRECTIONS   Write each personal pronoun from the following sentences. Then write the pronoun's number and, if the pronoun shows it, gender.

1. Simon and I entered the chess tournament after we had been in the Chess Club for six months.

2. Simon said it would be a good way to test our competence.

3. He's always looking for a challenge.

4. "Do you think it will be too hard for us?" I asked.

5. "I think you'll win a prize," he told me.

6. They gave out only three awards in each age group.

7. "You may all begin playing now," said the tournament director.

8. My chess partner has played with them for several years.

9. Her father taught us how to play chess.

10. Is the chess piece theirs?

Pronouns and Antecedents

An **antecedent** is the noun to which a **pronoun** refers. A pronoun agrees with its antecedent in number and gender. Number tells whether a pronoun is singular or plural. Gender tells whether a pronoun is masculine, feminine, or neuter.
Example:

> Leon asked *Anne* to tell *him* about some of *her* favorite books. (The singular masculine pronoun *him* refers to the antecedent *Leon*. The singular feminine pronoun *her* refers to the antecedent *Anne*.)

DIRECTIONS In each sentence, underline the personal pronoun and its antecedent. Then write the number and gender of the pronoun.

1. Travelers throughout the world are familiar with youth hostels and enjoy staying in them.

_____

2. American Youth Hostels, Inc., or AYH, began in 1934; it was organized to provide low-cost accommodations for travelers.

_____

3. Members of the organization can stay in hostels when they travel.

_____

4. Although hostels vary from country to country, they have basic features in common.

_____

5. Miranda stayed in hostels during a recent biking trip, and she introduced several friends to hosteling.

_____

6. Miranda brought photographs to class and showed them to several friends.

_____

7. Miranda wanted Miguel to see the pictures, but he seemed uninterested.

_____

8. Octavio and Carlos said they saved money by staying in hostels.

_____

9. A hostel can be an adventure; it can add to the enjoyment of a trip.

_____

10. Miranda's grandfather lives in England, and there is a hostel near where he lives.

_____

Subject and Object Pronouns

A **subject pronoun** can be used as a subject or a predicate nominative. *I, you, he, she, it, we,* and *they* are subject pronouns.
Examples:

> *I* have been reading about Marie Dorion. (subject)
> It is *I*. (predicate nominative)

An **object pronoun** can be used as a direct and an indirect object, and as an object of a preposition. *Me, you, him, her, it, us,* and *them* are object pronouns.
Examples:

> The coach saw *you*. (direct object)
> The coach gave *you* the notebook. (indirect object)
> The coach gave the notebook to *you*. (object of preposition)

DIRECTIONS ▸ **Underline the correct subject pronoun or object pronoun.**

1. Librarians read reviews of books before (they, them) buy (they, them).

2. You and (I, me) usually make our choices based on the title, the subject matter, and the author.

3. My friend often buys (I, me) books, and (I, me) always give (he, him) books for his birthday.

4. You or (I, me) might buy a book because of the book jacket.

5. Librarians sometimes adopt a wait-and-see attitude toward book purchasing since (they, them) have limited money to spend.

6. When our librarian does this, (she, her) is using our school's money wisely.

7. The librarian gave the books to (we, us).

8. (He, Him) is writing a book review on a new fiction novel.

9. The newspaper contacted (I, me) about writing a comic strip.

10. I wrote the story for (she, her).

DIRECTIONS ▸ **Rewrite the sentences, replacing each underlined phrase with a subject or an object pronoun.**

11. Our librarians want books that will stand the test of time.

_____

12. Ms. Delgado has provided us with many good books.

_____

13. You and I are the ones who benefit from careful book selection.

_____

14. The librarians gave the students a survey form to complete.

_____

15. They sent the overdue notice to you and me.

_____

Possessive Pronouns

A **possessive pronoun** shows ownership and replaces a possessive noun. *My, your, his, her, its, our,* and *their* are used before nouns.
Example:
    Jerome and I are learning about *our* ancestors.
Mine, yours, his, hers, ours, and *theirs* stand alone.
Example:
    This picture is *his.*

DIRECTIONS ▷ **Underline each possessive pronoun in these sentences.**

1. My English teacher tells me that Shakespeare wrote his plays between about 1590 and 1610.

2. If her information is correct, he wrote thirty-seven plays in just twenty years.

3. "Then I'd better get started on mine," I said. "I don't think I can write each of my plays in only six months."

4. I don't know what your ambition is, but mine is to be a playwright.

5. Perhaps yours is as exciting as mine.

6. I wonder whether Shakespeare knew his plays would one day be translated into Russian, German, and Spanish.

7. Did he know that the plays and their characters would reach as far away as Japan?

DIRECTIONS ▷ **Fill in the blank with an appropriate possessive pronoun.**

8. To some, Shakespeare is best known for _____ play *Romeo and Juliet.*

9. Romeo and Juliet could not marry because _____ two families were enemies.

10. Juliet had never disobeyed _____ father.

11. Romeo loved _____ parents, but he loved Juliet also.

12. Romeo asked _____ priest to marry them.

13. Friar Laurence did so because he thought _____ love might bring the two families together.

14. This marriage and _____ tragic outcome are well known all over the world.

15. *Romeo and Juliet* was recently performed in _____ town.

16. _____ father and I went to see it.

17. "Bats are not _____ favorite creatures," said Louis.

18. "They certainly aren't _____, either," agreed Tamara.

19. "Don't bats get into _____ hair?" asked Alan.

20. "Actually, they don't," said Ernie. "That's only one of several myths that have given bats _____ bad reputation."

Reflexive, Intensive, and Demonstrative Pronouns

A **reflexive pronoun** refers to the subject of a sentence. *Myself, yourself, himself, herself, itself, ourselves, yourselves,* and *themselves* are reflexive pronouns.
Example:
> One day, Marie found *herself* alone in the quiet forest.

An **intensive pronoun** emphasizes its antecedent. The intensive pronoun adds emphasis to a pronoun or noun already named.
Examples:
> I *myself* will go. They gave it to Henry *himself*.

A **demonstrative pronoun** points out a specific person, place, or thing. *This, that, these,* and *those* are demonstrative pronouns.
Examples:
> *This* is the correct answer. *That* is the incorrect answer.
> *These* are the correct answers. *Those* are the incorrect answers.

◎ ◎◎ ◎◎ ◎◎◎ ◎◎ ◎◎ ◎◎ ◎◎ ◎◎◎ ◎◎ ◎ ◎◎ ◎◎ ◎◎ ◎◎◎ ◎◎◎ ◎◎ ◎◎ ◎◎ ◎◎ ◎ ◎◎ ◎

DIRECTIONS ➤ Write the reflexive, intensive, or demonstrative pronoun from each sentence. Then write *reflexive, intensive,* or *demonstrative* to show what kind of pronoun it is.

1. Dad wanted to treat himself to a movie.
_____

2. "These are the movies I'd like to see," he said.
_____

3. "I think I'll just go by myself," he said.
_____

4. "The movie itself may not be great, but I'll enjoy the acting," Dad explained.
_____

5. "You go by yourself and we'll stay home," I said.
_____

6. "Are you sure you can entertain yourselves?"
_____

7. "I think that is something we can do."
_____

DIRECTIONS ➤ Write a reflexive, intensive, or demonstrative pronoun to complete each sentence. Write *reflexive, intensive,* or *demonstrative* to show what kind of pronoun you added.

8. After Dad left, I got _____ a bowl of trail mix. _____

9. "Would you like some of _____?" I asked my older brother. _____

10. "No, thanks," he said. "I don't want any of _____, but I would like some fruit.

   Shall I get it _____?" _____

◎ ◎◎ ◎◎ ◎◎◎ ◎◎ ◎◎ ◎◎ ◎◎◎ ◎◎ ◎◎ ◎◎ ◎◎◎ ◎◎ ◎◎ ◎◎ ◎◎ ◎ ◎◎ ◎◎

Indefinite Pronouns

An **indefinite pronoun** does not refer to a specific person, place, or thing.
Example:
>*Somebody* will do the work.

The indefinite pronouns *anybody, anyone, anything, each, everyone, everybody, everything, nobody, no one, nothing, one, somebody, someone,* and *something* are singular. They take singular verbs.
Example:
>*Everyone is* coming to the play.

The indefinite pronouns *both, few, many, several,* and *some* are plural. They take plural verbs.
Example:
>*Many are* coming to the play.

Indefinite pronouns agree with their possessive pronouns in number and gender.
Example:
>*Each* of the boys sent *his* invitations.

DIRECTIONS ▷ **Write the word in parentheses that correctly completes each sentence.**

1. Last night, everyone _____ putting on a costume.
   (was, were)

2. All of the spectators _____ waiting for the play.
   (was, were)

3. Several of the performers couldn't put on _____ makeup.
   (her, their)

4. Some of the younger children _____ crying.
   (was, were)

5. One of the first-grade teachers _____ comforting the unhappy children.
   (was, were)

6. Both of the stars had forgotten _____ lines.
   (his, her, their)

7. When the final curtain fell, however, most of the spectators had enjoyed _____
   (himself, herself, themselves)

   and _____ smiling.
   (was, were)

8. Several of the girls gave _____ teacher a bouquet of flowers.
   (her, their)

9. Few _____ in a hurry to leave the auditorium.
   (was, were)

10. Each of the performers _____ given a small gift.
    (was, were)

11. No one _____ to go home empty-handed.
    (was, were)

12. _____ anybody have a camera?
    (Do, Does)

Interrogative and Relative Pronouns

Use an **interrogative pronoun** to begin a question. *Who, whom,* and *whose* are interrogative pronouns.
Example:
> *Whom* did you see?

Use a **relative pronoun** to link a group of words to a preceding noun or pronoun. *Who, which,* and *that* are relative pronouns.
Example:
> Give me the book *that* you selected.

DIRECTIONS Underline the relative pronouns and interrogative pronouns in these sentences. Identify each by writing *relative pronoun* or *interrogative pronoun*. Write the antecedent for each relative pronoun.

1. We need a class president who is a true leader.

   _____

2. Some candidates simply state platitudes that the students want to hear.

   _____

3. Who will have the courage to voice the message that we need?

   _____

4. We have had strong class leaders in the past, but to whom will the mantle of leadership be passed?

   _____

5. A candidate whose message is true and who delivers it with conviction can convince others to make the hard choices for our class.

   _____

DIRECTIONS Rewrite each sentence to correct errors in the use of relative pronouns and interrogative pronouns. If the sentence is correct, write *correct*.

6. Who opened the ballot box?

   _____

7. Was it the person whom spoke to us earlier?

   _____

8. Who can I trust with the ballot box?

   _____

9. Whom will the voters choose?

   _____

10. They whom are here will vote.

    _____

Verbs

A **verb** is a word that expresses action or being. The main word in the predicate of a sentence is a verb.
Example:
> Garth *talks* constantly about the Middle Ages.

An **action verb** tells what the subject does, did, or will do.
Example:
> Many tourists *visit* castles in Europe.

A **linking verb** links the subject of a sentence with a word in the predicate that describes the subject.
Example:
> Garth's stories about castles *are* wonderful.

DIRECTIONS Identify the verb in each sentence. Label each verb *action* or *linking*.

1. Pirates left Lord and Lady Greystoke on a primitive island.

2. Lady Greystoke, a young and intelligent woman, felt challenged.

3. Together they made a sturdy cabin out of hand-hewn logs and clay.

4. One day, a large leopard surprised Lord Greystoke in the woods.

5. Greystoke attacked his foe with an ax, the only weapon available.

6. Lady Greystoke appeared calm.

7. Picking up a firearm, she shot the leopard.

8. As a young boy, writer and teacher Richard Rodríguez lived in two different worlds.

9. Richard's family spoke mostly Spanish at home.

10. He entered first grade at a school in Sacramento, California.

11. As a small child, Richard never heard his name in English.

12. School was an often confusing and painful experience for him.

13. Richard nevertheless became a very successful student.

14. Years later, he graduated from Stanford University.

15. Then he earned a doctoral degree in English.

Main Verbs and Helping Verbs

A **verb phrase** is made up of a **main verb**, the most important verb in a verb phrase, and one or more **helping verbs**.
Examples:
> My teacher *will tell* us about Peru.
> Mr. Vargas *has been living* here for twelve years.

DIRECTIONS ▸ Write the verb phrases from each sentence. Circle the main verb.

1. Within the next decade, we may be traveling to other planets.

   _____

2. One of the first stops could be Phobus, a moon of Mars.

   _____

3. Discussions have already been held among scientists in several countries.

   _____

4. In the past, such joint ventures were thought difficult.

   _____

5. However, many people have changed their thinking and are now rearranging their priorities.

   _____

6. Joint ventures could result in increased understanding between people of different backgrounds.

   _____

7. Mother otters will protect their young carefully.

   _____

8. In case of danger, a mother will dive below the surface.

   _____

9. People on otter-watching expeditions should keep their boats a good distance away from mothers and pups.

   _____

DIRECTIONS ▸ Rewrite each sentence, adding one or more helping verbs to the main verb in parentheses.

10. Peaceful cooperation in outer space (take) people on fantastic adventures in the very near future.

    _____

11. By the year 2020, scientists (live) and (work) on Phobus.

    _____

12. Perhaps people (learn) to get along when they must live together far from Earth.

    _____

13. LaKeesha (admire) the sea otters at the aquarium.

    _____

Principal Parts of Regular Verbs

The four basic forms of a verb are its **principal parts**. These forms are the **present, present participle, past,** and **past participle**.

Examples:

Present	Present Participle	Past	Past Participle
play	(is, are, am) playing	played	(has, have, had) played
move	(is, are, am) moving	moved	(has, have, had) moved

DIRECTIONS ▷ Write the verb or verb phrase from each sentence. Then identify the principal part of the main verb by writing *present, present participle, past,* or *past participle.*

1. Rebecca and her husband traveled to Utah.

_____

_____

2. He had taken the same route twice before.

_____

_____

3. She called to her husband.

_____

_____

4. "The sheep are acting very thirsty."

_____

_____

5. Aaron had worried about the lack of water.

_____

_____

6. He shouted encouragement to her.

_____

_____

7. "I see a river in the distance."

_____

_____

8. "We are camping there for the night."

_____

_____

9. Hurricanes usually form over the ocean.

_____

_____

10. In 1992, Hurricane Albert caused great destruction in Florida and in other parts of the South.

_____

_____

11. Fortunately, meteorologists are now predicting the paths of hurricanes quite accurately.

_____

_____

DIRECTIONS ▷ On the lines below, write the principal parts of each of the following verbs: *walk, stop, hike, cry, arrive.*

12. Today we _____

13. Today we are _____

14. Yesterday we _____

15. Once we had _____

Principal Parts of Irregular Verbs

Irregular verbs do not have *ed* or *d* added to form the past and the past participle.
Examples:

Present	Present Participle	Past	Past Participle
drink	(is, are, am) drinking	drank	(has, have, had) drunk
begin	(is, are, am) beginning	began	(has, have, had) begun

The **past participle** of some irregular verbs is formed by adding *n, en,* or *ne* to the present or the past.
Examples:

Present	Present Participle	Past	Past Participle
fly	(is, are, am) flying	flew	(has, have, had) flown
grow	(is, are, am) growing	grew	(has, have, had) grown

DIRECTIONS ▷ Write the correct principal part of the verb in parentheses. Then identify the principle part that you used.

1. To get to the island, the boys had _____ before dawn.
   (leave)
   _____

2. An hour, later they _____ themselves at the quiet cove Henry had described.
   (find)
   _____

3. "It is _____ light," said Josh. _____
   (become)

4. Individual rays of sunlight _____ through the jungle that _____
   (shine)   (begin)
   some thirty feet beyond them. _____

5. Suddenly an animal _____ out of the jungle and _____ toward them.
   (burst)   (spring)
   _____

6. "I warned you about the boars!" yelled Henry as he _____ toward a tall tree.
   (run)
   _____

7. "Either you didn't, or I had _____ them out of my mind," yelled Josh, jumping
   (put)
   back into the boat. _____

8. "But don't worry. I'll just sit here until I have _____ of how to help you."
   (think)
   _____

9. Have you ever _____ through a straw? _____
   (drink)

10. Martin Stone _____ out this invention in 1888.
    (bring)
    _____

Principal Parts of Irregular Verbs, page 2

DIRECTIONS Use the correct past participle of each verb in parentheses.

1. The leaves have _____, and the wind has _____ them all into a
   (fall)   (blow)
   corner of the yard.

2. I have _____ my typewriter and holed up in my study.
   (take)

3. The weather has _____ me an idea for a story.
   (give)

4. I have _____ ideas like this before, but _____ them before I had a
   (get)   (forget)
   chance to work with them.

5. When I have _____ this story, I will feel that I have _____ more
   (write)   (grow)
   disciplined as a writer.

DIRECTIONS On the lines below, write the principal parts of each of the following verbs:
break, fly, wear, go, rise.

6. Today we _____

7. Today we are _____

8. Yesterday we _____

9. Once we had _____

DIRECTIONS Write the past and the past participle for each verb.

	Present	Past	Past Participle
10.	run	_____	_____
11.	say	_____	_____
12.	tell	_____	_____
13.	write	_____	_____
14.	teach	_____	_____
15.	swim	_____	_____
16.	build	_____	_____
17.	speak	_____	_____
18.	hide	_____	_____

Be, Have, and Do

Remember that some irregular verbs do not form the past or past participle by adding *ed*.
Examples:

Present	Past	Past Participle
am, are, is	was, were	been
have, has	had	had
do, does	did	done

Remember that the irregular verbs **be, have,** and **do** can be used as main verbs or as helping verbs.
Examples:

    I *am* at school.
    I *am taking* my books home.

Use the correct contractions for the verbs **be, have,** and **do**.
Examples:

    aren't, haven't, doesn't

DIRECTIONS ▷ **Write the correct contraction for each sentence.**

1. I _____ care much for sports.
   (don't, doesn't)

2. My brother _____ like most sports, either.
   (don't, doesn't)

3. He _____ played on many teams.
   (haven't, hasn't)

4. I guess we _____ very athletic.
   (aren't, isn't)

5. Most of our friends _____ agree with us.
   (don't, doesn't)

6. Jerry _____ any stronger than I am, but he's terrific at most games.
   (aren't, isn't)

7. Carla _____ won any of her recent tennis matches, but she still enjoys the game.
   (haven't, hasn't)

8. My friends _____ understand why I _____ join some of their teams.
   (don't, doesn't)   (don't, doesn't)

DIRECTIONS ▷ **Complete each sentence by using the correct form of the verb in parentheses.**

9. Our school sports program _____ cut recently.
   (was, were)

10. Many people believe that sports _____ as important as academics.
    (am, are, is)

11. Now Sara, a fifth-grader, _____ only one opportunity to play soccer.
    (has, have)

12. Will our school have _____ her a disservice if it _____ not offer
    (do, did, done)   (do, does)

her a chance at team sports?

Verb Tenses

There are six tenses for every verb: **present, past, future, present perfect, past perfect,** and **future perfect.**

Examples:

Present	Past	Future	Present Perfect	Past Perfect	Future Perfect
laugh	laughed	will laugh	has laughed	had laughed	will have laughed
sit	sat	will sit	has sat	had sat	will have sat

DIRECTIONS ▷ **Underline the verb or verb phrase in each sentence and write its tense on the line.**

1. Since the early part of this century, movies have been a major source of entertainment.

   _____

2. Studios in countries throughout the world produced silent films. _____

3. Some people consider silent films amateurish. _____

4. Apparently these people have seen only the bad films. _____

5. Long before "talkies," silent film directors like D. W. Griffith had made masterpieces. _____

6. The word *hurricane* came into English from the Taino word *hurakán*. _____

7. For the Arawakan Indians of the Caribbean, this word meant "big wind." _____

8. When will winds of hurricane force strike the United States again? _____

9. In the late summer and early fall of every year, weather forecasters wrestle with this question.

   _____

10. Hurricanes normally deposit large quantities of rain on an area. _____

11. However, strong winds will do the greatest damage. _____

12. Hurricanes weaken over land. _____

13. Before the 1990s, few boys had enrolled in home economics courses. _____

14. Now, however, the situation has changed. _____

15. Many boys have found home economics classes useful and interesting. _____

16. Before the changes, some boys had thought of home economics as a girls' subject. _____

17. Until recently, they had not appreciated the new focus of many courses in this area. _____

18. Many of today's schools have created an interest in practical studies. _____

19. Soon the course titles *Work and Family Studies* and *Life Management Education* will have

    replaced *Home Economics* at some schools. _____

20. By the time today's students grow up, the roles of men and women in the family will probably

    have changed greatly. _____

Verb Tenses, page 2

DIRECTIONS ▷ The following sentences contain errors in the use of present, past, and future tenses. Underline the incorrect verb or verb phrase. Then write the correct verb form on the line.

1. In the past, weather officials will give hurricanes the names of girls. _____

2. For example, Gloria, a very destructive storm, will strike in 1985. _____

3. Now, however, officials also used boys' names for the storms. _____

4. Today, they alternated boys' and girls' names in alphabetical order—for example, Alberto, Beryl, Chris, Debby, and Ernesto. _____

5. Which names were on the list next year? _____

6. My name, Wynona, was unlikely to be used. _____

7. Maybe someday my friend Zilpha and I shared our names with future hurricanes. _____

8. Had the weather officials used all of the names by 2099? _____

9. Naming hurricanes made them seem alive, doesn't it? _____

10. Perhaps officials give hurricanes numbers someday. _____

DIRECTIONS ▷ Write each sentence, using the verb and the tense given in parentheses.

11. Many social changes (redefine) men's roles in the family. (present perfect)

_____

_____

12. Before the 1970s, few men (study) cooking in school. (past perfect)

_____

_____

13. Women traditionally (have) most of the responsibility for keeping house and raising children. (present perfect)

_____

_____

14. The new courses in this area, introduced in recent years, (appeal) to more and more boys. (present perfect)

_____

_____

15. By the year 2025, many men as well as women (use) these skills at home and in their careers. (future perfect)

_____

_____

Tense Changes

The **tense** of a verb shows time. Remember to keep verb tenses consistent within sentences and from sentence to sentence. Change verb tenses only to show that the time of events changes.
Examples:
Dena *tells* funny stories, and everyone *laughs*. (present tense)
She *told* a funny story last night, and everyone *laughed*. (past tense)

DIRECTIONS ▷ **Complete the sentences, using the correct form of the verbs in parentheses.**

1. Although English is the dominant language in both England and the United States, there
   _____ (be) differences in both accent and word usage.

2. Once when someone _____ (ask) if I wanted biscuits, I fully _____
   (expect) the baking soda variety, perhaps hot with butter and jam.

3. As I was hungry, what I got _____ (be) quite a disappointment.

4. If I had _____ (know) then what I _____ (know) now, I would have
   _____ (expect) plain cookies, not American-style biscuits.

5. As I _____ (learn) to speak the King's English, thumbtacks became "drawing
   pins"; an elevator _____ (become) a "lift"; children in the primary years
   _____ (become) "infants"; and a line _____ (become) a "queue."

6. Mr. Lee has just now _____ (start) the rehearsal.

7. There had been a delay because a meeting had _____ (run) long.

8. Amy, Bianca, Joey, and I have _____ (watch) three skits already.

9. In a moment, we will have _____ (wait) for a full hour.

10. Mr. Lee _____ (have) worked with us for a week now.

11. Before these rehearsals, I _____ (do) not realize that he was so funny.

12. By next fall, he will have _____ (coach) here for ten years.

13. I _____ (see) him talking to the principal an hour ago.

DIRECTIONS ▷ **Rewrite each sentence to correct inconsistent verb tenses.**

14. If there are not some embarrassing mix-ups, I would have found relearning the language a painless
    experience. _____
    _____

15. After a while, I begin to enjoy the lilting way the voices of my British friends rose and fall.
    _____

Progressive Forms of Verbs

The **progressive form** of a verb shows continuing action. A form of the verb *be* plus the present participle forms the progressive. (The present participle is the form of the verb ending in *ing*.)
Examples:

Present Progressive
I am walking. You are walking. He is walking.
Past Progressive
I was walking. You were walking. He was walking.
Future Progressive
I will be walking. You will be walking. He will be walking.
Present Perfect Progressive
I have been walking. You have been walking. He has been walking.
Past Perfect Progressive
I had been walking. You had been walking. He had been walking.
Future Perfect Progressive
I will have been walking. You will have been walking. He will have been walking.

◎◎◎ ◎◎ ◎◎ ◎◎ ◎◎◎ ◎◎ ◎◎ ◎◎ ◎◎◎ ◎◎ ◎◎ ◎◎ ◎◎◎ ◎◎ ◎◎ ◎◎ ◎◎ ◎◎ ◎◎

DIRECTIONS ▷ **Write the tense of each progressive form given. Then write a sentence using that progressive form.**

1. (is drawing) _____

2. (had been running) _____

3. (will be helping) _____

4. (has been speaking) _____

5. (will have been discussing) _____

6. (were anticipating) _____

DIRECTIONS ▷ **Rewrite each sentence. Replace the underlined verb with a progressive form of the verb.**

7. For eight years, Marlene <u>has won</u> ribbons for her baked goods at the state fair.

_____

8. Before that, she <u>had baked</u> only for her family.

_____

9. Last month Marlene <u>thought</u> about what to enter this year.

_____

10. This year she <u>will bake</u> pies, cakes, and breads.

_____

Direct Objects

The noun or pronoun that receives the action of the verb is the **direct object**. A direct object tells who or what receives the action.
Example:
    Bobby loved his *brother*.
Compound direct objects are formed when two or more objects receive the same action.
Examples:
    Bobby loved his brother. Bobby loved his sister.
    Bobby loved his *brother* and his *sister*.

DIRECTIONS Write the simple subject, the verb, and the direct object from each sentence. If there is no direct object, write *no direct object*.

1. Penguins live almost exclusively on small ice islands in the Antarctic.

2. Penguins like the cold climate.

3. Penguins use their wings not for flying but for swimming.

4. A female penguin lays a single egg.

5. The male penguin tucks this inside a special fold of skin near his feet to keep it warm until hatching time.

6. Certain penguins return to the same spot every year.

7. Have you read any books about penguins?

DIRECTIONS Combine the sentences in each pair. Punctuate the sentences correctly.

8. Most people like these funny, tuxedoed birds. Most people like their waddling walk.

9. Sea World in San Diego, California, built a climate-controlled ice island for Emperor penguins. Sea World built a large icy pool for the Emperor penguins.

10. Most penguins eat small fish and squid. Most penguins eat shrimp.

Indirect Objects

An **indirect object** tells to whom or for whom the action of the verb is done.
Example:

Jack showed the *dog* kindness.

DIRECTIONS ▷ For each sentence write the simple subject, the verb, the indirect object, and the direct object, in that order.

1. Visits to state reserves offer many people views of animals in their natural habitats.

2. Animals in the wild can bring city folk much enjoyment.

3. Reserves and wildlife refuges also afford animals protection from poachers and pollution.

4. Some reserves offer visitors guided tours.

5. Guidebooks and occasional special programs give nature hikers additional information.

6. I offered the dogs treats.

7. I gave each dog a warning about politeness.

DIRECTIONS ▷ Rewrite each sentence, replacing the underlined phrase with an indirect object.

8. The university offered internships at a marine reserve <u>to juniors</u>.

9. One reserve gave a job observing the habits of sea lions <u>to a student</u>.

10. At the end of the semester, the student handed a fascinating report on the feeding of sea lions <u>to her professor</u>.

DIRECTIONS ▷ Expand each sentence so that it will have an indirect object as well as a direct object. Write the new sentences.

11. My friend asked questions about the first meeting.

12. I told the facts.

Predicate Nominatives

> A **predicate nominative** is a noun or pronoun that follows a linking verb and renames the subject.
> *Example:*
>   Lassie <u>has been</u> a *celebrity* for decades.

 **DIRECTIONS** Underline all the predicate nominatives in each sentence. Then draw an arrow from each predicate nominative to the subject it refers to.

1. Truck drivers are one link between producers and consumers in the United States.

2. A requirement for every professional driver is hard work.

3. Another essential qualification is commitment.

4. A determination to drive safely is also a necessity.

5. Controlling a huge truck is no easy task.

6. The most dangerous vehicles of all are bobtail tractors, lightweight rigs, and hazardous materials tankers.

7. Stormy weather may be a trucker's enemy.

8. The most hazardous conditions are often rain, ice, and desert heat.

9. Speeding is often a cause of trucking accidents.

10. Another important cause of accidents may be a lapse of attention.

11. For most truckers, driving is a difficult, tiring job.

12. For a few, it is an enjoyable diversion.

13. Accidents are the nightmares of all truckers.

14. Big-rig accidents are often deadly accidents.

15. "Rinty" was a puppy when he came to America.

16. His owner and trainer was Corporal Lee Duncan.

17. Rin Tin Tin became a star.

18. She is still an inspiration today.

19. A Halloween pumpkin is a jack-o-lantern.

20. A pumpkin is really a squash.

Transitive and Intransitive Verbs

> A **transitive verb** is an action verb that is followed by a noun or pronoun that receives the action. Therefore, all transitive verbs have a direct object.
> *Example:*
>   I *know* the story.
> An **intransitive verb** includes all linking verbs and any action verbs that do not take an object.
> *Example:*
>   Greyfriars Bobby *was* a Skye terrier. "Auld Jack" Gray *died*.

DIRECTIONS Write the action verb in each sentence and, if there is one, the direct object. Then identify the verb as *transitive* or *intransitive*.

1. Throughout history, men and women have traveled in search of adventure.

2. Their discoveries have increased knowledge about our world.

3. Centuries ago, Marco Polo brought tales of the Orient to people in his country.

4. Even in recent decades, explorers have ventured into unmapped areas.

5. Today, organizations such as the Sierra Club offer members expeditions once available only to explorers.

6. People will never lose their interest in exploring the unknown.

7. Astronauts, scientists, and others have already traveled into space.

8. Native American myths and folktales often use Coyote as the main character.

9. Typically, Coyote tricks his opponents in the stories.

10. In one important Navajo tale, Coyote creates the world.

11. In other stories, he slays monsters through trickery.

12. However, Coyote's tricks sometimes backfire.

13. Modern writers have written poems and stories about this fascinating creature.

Active and Passive Voice

> **Voice** is that property of a verb that indicates whether the subject of the verb is performing or receiving an action.
> When a verb is in the **active voice**, the subject performs the action.
> *Examples:*
>   He wrote the letter. They are working in the city.
> When a verb is in the **passive voice**, the subject receives the action.
> *Examples:*
>   A soldier was awarded a medal. We were impressed by the beauty of the performance.
> Use the active voice more than the passive voice when you write since active verbs are stronger than passive verbs.

DIRECTIONS > Rewrite each sentence in the active voice.

1. Surfing has been enjoyed by young men and women for many years.

   _____

   _____

2. In many parts of the country, the sport was popularized by singing groups.

   _____

3. Surfing music was played by numerous groups.

   _____

4. Many teenagers were introduced to surfing by the music of these groups.

   _____

5. These songs are still enjoyed by many people.

   _____

6. The waves are carefully watched by surfers all along the coast.

   _____

7. The exhilaration and sense of freedom that come from riding the waves are enjoyed by surfers.

   _____

8. The walls of the room were almost covered with posters of musicians.

   _____

9. A trade agreement with Mexico has been approved by the Senate.

   _____

10. Most of their spare time was spent on the farm.

   _____

Easily Confused Verb Pairs

Remember always to check troublesome verb pairs. To use them correctly, study which words should have or usually have direct objects.

Use **lie** when you mean "rest" or "recline." It does not take an object.
Example:
> You can *lie* here for a while.

Use **lay** when you mean "place something in a reclining position." *Lay* does take an object.
Example:
> *Lay* the books on the desk.

Use **sit** when you mean "rest, as in a chair." *Sit* does not take an object.
Example:
> Please *sit* down.

Use **set** when you mean "put something in a certain place." *Set* does take an object.
Example:
> My sister *set* the flowers on the table.

Use **rise** when you mean "get up" or "move higher." *Rise* does not take an object.
Example:
> Smoke from the fire *rises*.

Use **raise** when you mean "lift something up." *Raise* does take an object.
Example:
> My grandmother *raises* the window slightly.

Use **leave** when you mean "to depart" or "to allow something to remain where it is." *Leave* may take an object.
Example:
> She did *leave* home.

Use **let** when you mean "to allow" or "to permit." *Let* may take an object.
Example:
> Angelina *lets* me help.

DIRECTIONS Choose the correct verb to complete each sentence. Write it in the blank.

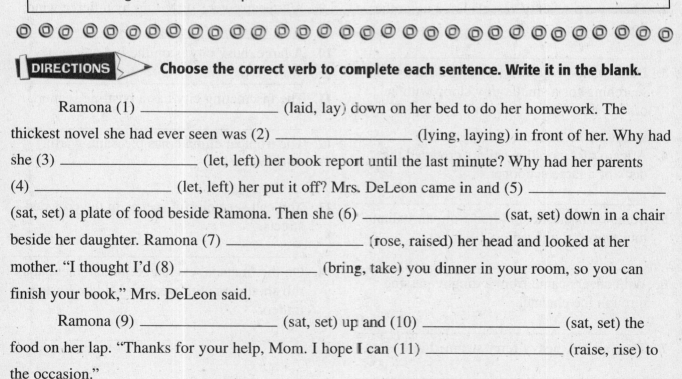

Ramona (1) _____ (laid, lay) down on her bed to do her homework. The thickest novel she had ever seen was (2) _____ (lying, laying) in front of her. Why had she (3) _____ (let, left) her book report until the last minute? Why had her parents (4) _____ (let, left) her put it off? Mrs. DeLeon came in and (5) _____ (sat, set) a plate of food beside Ramona. Then she (6) _____ (sat, set) down in a chair beside her daughter. Ramona (7) _____ (rose, raised) her head and looked at her mother. "I thought I'd (8) _____ (bring, take) you dinner in your room, so you can finish your book," Mrs. DeLeon said.

Ramona (9) _____ (sat, set) up and (10) _____ (sat, set) the food on her lap. "Thanks for your help, Mom. I hope I can (11) _____ (raise, rise) to the occasion."

Adjectives

An **adjective** modifies a noun or a pronoun. Adjectives tell *what kind, how many,* or *which one.*
Example:
  Three adults and *four* cubs rested there.
A and *an* are **indefinite articles**. They can refer to any person, place, thing, or idea. *The* is a **definite article**; it refers to a particular person, place, thing, or idea.
Example:
  A banana and *an* apple are on *the* table.
A **proper adjective** is formed from a proper noun. A proper adjective begins with a capital letter.
Examples:
  African history, *Scottish* bagpipes, *Thai* cuisine
Use a comma between two or more adjectives if each modifies the noun by itself or if the order can be reversed.
Example:
  The sweet, red strawberries were delicious.

DIRECTIONS Read each sentence. Underline the adjectives and circle the articles. Identify any proper adjectives by drawing two lines under them. Then write the words that the adjectives modify.

1. The small boats at the marina bobbed in the rough water.

   _____

2. There were seventy vessels lined up at the dock.

   _____

3. Dana wandered down the long dock, searching for a small, gray sloop with an orange jib.

   _____

4. A team of Australian sailors crowded the deck of a large schooner.

   _____

5. Some enthusiastic children from an Italian tour waved to the sailors.

   _____

6. Wild cheers came from a dinghy passing through the channel.

   _____

7. Then an old, heavy ferry steamed into view.

   _____

8. The dark, murky water obscured the bottom of the channel.

   _____

9. Whitecaps were stirred up by a fierce wind.

   _____

10. A large, busy city is on the Indian coast.

   _____

11. The fascinating city has a bustling seaport.

   _____

12. The tropical climate has pleasant, warm, salty breezes.

   _____

13. You can see colorful scenes in the crowded streets.

   _____

14. On the financial exchange, Indian merchants rub shoulders with wealthy Middle Eastern traders.

   _____

Predicate Adjectives

A **predicate adjective** is an adjective that follows a linking verb and describes the subject of the sentence.
Example:
> Rin Tin Tin <u>was</u> *famous* in Hollywood, too.

◎ ◎ ◎◎ ◎◎ ◎◎◎◎ ◎ ◎◎ ◎◎ ◎ ◎◎◎ ◎◎ ◎ ◎◎◎ ◎ ◎◎ ◎◎ ◎ ◎◎◎ ◎◎ ◎ ◎◎◎ ◎ ◎◎ ◎ ◎ ◎ ◎

DIRECTIONS ▷ Write *predicate adjective* or *predicate nominative* (see p. 28) to identify the underlined word or words in each sentence.

1. The pit crew felt <u>hot</u> and <u>grimy</u>.

_____

2. Perhaps their driver's car was a <u>lemon</u>.

_____

3. Those odd puffs from the engine were certainly <u>smoke</u>.

_____

4. Now the outcome of the race seemed <u>uncertain</u>.

_____

5. Of course, the crew's driver was a <u>professional</u>.

_____

6. However, he appeared <u>worried</u> about the race, too.

_____

7. Those noises from the engine were <u>ominous</u>.

_____

8. If he lost the race, the driver would be <u>angry</u>.

_____

9. In the last four races, his old rival had been the <u>winner</u>.

_____

10. He felt <u>frustrated</u> by his recent failures.

_____

11. The shadow clock may have been the earliest <u>device</u> for keeping time.

_____

12. In its simplest form, this instrument was a <u>stick</u> in the ground.

_____

13. The sundial was another ancient <u>instrument</u> for measuring time.

_____

14. Water clocks were also <u>common</u> in ancient Greece.

_____

15. In an hourglass, the flow of sand was the <u>measure</u> of time.

_____

16. Devices for keeping time gradually became more <u>complex</u>.

_____

17. In the fourteenth century, the first mechanical clocks probably seemed <u>magical</u>.

_____

18. These clocks were <u>heavy</u> and <u>awkward</u>.

_____

19. Early mechanical clocks had only one hand, and many were <u>inaccurate</u>.

_____

Comparisons with Adjectives

The **positive form** of an adjective is used when no comparison is being made.
Examples:

old   wonderful   imaginative

How *old* the Inca empire seems to us today!

The **comparative form** of an adjective is used to compare two items. Form the comparative of most one-syllable adjectives by adding *er*. For most adjectives with two or more syllables, add the word *more* before the adjective.
Examples:

older   more wonderful   more imaginative

The Aztec empire is *older* than the Inca empire.

The **superlative form** of an adjective is used to compare three or more items. Form the superlative of most one-syllable adjectives by adding *est*. For most adjectives with two or more syllables, add the word *most* before the adjective.
Examples:

oldest   most wonderful   most imaginative

The Mayan empire is the *oldest* one in the Americas.

DIRECTIONS Underline the comparing adjective in each sentence. Then write *comparative* or *superlative* to identify its degree of comparison.

1. The giant sequoia is the tallest tree on the earth. _____

2. A giant sequoia may be taller than a skyscraper. _____

3. These magnificent trees are among the oldest living things on the earth. _____

4. The General Grant sequoia is one of the most important tourist attractions in Yosemite National Park. _____

5. Many tourists consider a grove of giant sequoias the most impressive sight in the state.

_____

6. Cones from the redwood sequoia are larger than those from the giant sequoia. _____

DIRECTIONS Rewrite each sentence, using the correct form of the adjective.

7. Logging is the most large industry in Oregon.

_____

8. The loggers' organization is more powerfuller than many other groups.

_____

9. We are learning to be more carefuller of our forests than we once were.

_____

10. Unfortunately, the world's forests are more small than they were even a few decades ago.

_____

Comparisons with Adjectives, page 2

 **DIRECTIONS** Underline each positive form of an adjective once. Underline each comparative form twice and each superlative form three times. Do not underline articles or demonstrative adjectives.

1. California, which stretches for hundreds of miles down the Pacific coast, is more populous than any other state in the nation.

2. Some people say that San Francisco is the most beautiful city in America.

3. One of the most picturesque neighborhoods in this hilly city by the bay is Chinatown.

4. The best time to visit San Francisco is in early autumn, when the chilly fog does not blanket the city.

5. Los Angeles is probably the most important city in America for entertainment.

6. Who hasn't heard of fabulous Hollywood?

7. According to many professionals, the University of California at Los Angeles offers the most useful training for filmmakers.

8. Between California's two great cities lie miles of spectacular coastline.

9. Most parks in California are more crowded on holidays than on weekends.

10. Some neighborhoods of San Diego have a Mexican flavor; the Mexican border is very close to the city.

DIRECTIONS Write the correct form of the adjective in parentheses.

11. Yosemite is not the _____ national park, but it is one of the most spectacular.
    (old)

12. It is _____ than I ever imagined.
    (beautiful)

13. Yosemite Falls is the _____ series of waterfalls in North America.
    (high)

14. The conservationist John Muir had _____ influence than anyone else in
    (much)
    persuading Congress to declare Yosemite a national park.

15. During summer, Yosemite is one of America's _____ national park.
    (busy)

Irregular Comparisons with Adjectives

Some adjectives have special forms for comparing.
Examples:

Positive	Comparative	Superlative
good	better	best
bad	worse	worst
much	more	most
little	less	least

◎◎◎ ◎◎◎ ◎◎◎◎ ◎◎◎◎ ◎◎◎◎ ◎◎◎◎ ◎◎◎◎ ◎◎◎◎ ◎◎◎◎ ◎◎◎◎ ◎◎◎ ◎

DIRECTIONS ▷ **Write each sentence, using the correct form of comparison.**

1. Reading ingredient labels is the _____ way to evaluate prepared foods.
   (more best, best)

2. Some labels may boast foods with _____ sodium.
   (less, fewer)

3. Other labels advertise foods with _____ calories.
   (less, fewer)

4. Many nutritionists say that sugar is the _____ additive.
   (most worst, worst)

5. For many consumers, no-salt foods have the _____ appeal.
   (most least, least)

6. Usually, foods with _____ salt are _____ for you.
   (fewer, less)   (more better, better)

DIRECTIONS ▷ **Write *positive*, *comparative*, or *superlative* to identify the underlined adjective in each sentence.**

7. Many people think that the <u>best</u> foods are homemade. _____

8. They think that the <u>fewer</u> unnatural ingredients we add to our food, the healthier we will be.

   _____

9. Some think that <u>perfect</u> foods come directly from the earth to the table. _____

10. Other people think that the <u>less</u> work a meal involves, the better it tastes. _____

11. Almost everyone agrees that fresh water tastes <u>good</u>. _____

12. Drinking cool water directly from a spring is a <u>unique</u> experience. _____

13. A drink of water will almost always make you feel <u>better</u>. _____

14. Painting the faces was the <u>worst</u> part of the job. _____

15. I used <u>more</u> paint than my partner did. _____

◎◎◎ ◎◎◎ ◎◎◎ ◎◎◎◎ ◎◎◎ ◎◎◎◎ ◎◎◎ ◎◎◎◎ ◎◎◎ ◎◎◎ ◎◎◎◎ ◎◎◎ ◎

Irregular Comparisons with Adjectives, page 2

> **DIRECTIONS** > **Write the form of the adjective in parentheses that correctly completes each sentence.**

1. We were all competing to see who could create the (good) poster about an ancient civilization.

   _____

2. The Great Wall of China wasn't a (bad) idea at all! _____

3. This poster is definitely (good) than last year's winner. _____

4. Ms. Martin is feeling (good) than she did yesterday, rather than (bad), so she'll judge the posters this afternoon. _____

5. This contest has been (much) fun than anything else I've done this month. _____

6. In fact, it may be the (good) activity of the year. _____

7. The (good) thing to do on a trip is to travel light. _____

8. Less baggage is (good) than (much) baggage. _____

9. Of these two brochures, this one is (bad). _____

10. There are (much) pictures than words. _____

11. I was sick on the first day, but now I feel (good). _____

12. The cruise with the (little) cost of all is to Aruba. _____

> **DIRECTIONS** > **Write a review of a local restaurant, evaluating its food, service, and atmosphere. Use comparative forms of adjectives such as *good*, *bad*, and *little*.**

_____

_____

_____

_____

_____

_____

_____

_____

_____

_____

_____

Other Parts of Speech as Adjectives

A pronoun, noun, or verb can also function as an adjective.
Examples:
> *These* are very ripe bananas. (pronoun)
> *These* bananas are too ripe. (adjective)
> The *stone* looks impressive. (noun)
> The *stone* house looks impressive. (adjective)
> The water is *running* down the street. (verb)
> The *running* water pooled in the street. (adjective)

DIRECTIONS ▷ Write *adjective, pronoun, noun,* or *verb* to identify the underlined word in each sentence.

1. It was difficult to tell <u>which</u> radio was playing. _____

2. "<u>Which</u> is on now?" the customer asked a sales clerk. _____

3. Music from TVs and stereos was <u>blaring</u> through the store. _____

4. The <u>blaring</u> music bothered some of the customers. _____

5. The sales clerk led the customer to a <u>listening</u> room. _____

6. Other customers were <u>listening</u> in another tiny room. _____

7. "<u>All</u> of these buttons confuse me," complained the customer. _____

8. "Not <u>all</u> radios have so many buttons," explained the clerk. _____

9. <u>Several</u> portable radios were on display. _____

10. The clerk brought <u>several</u> to the customer. _____

11. "<u>This</u> is too heavy," remarked the customer. _____

12. "<u>This</u> radio is smaller," said the clerk. _____

13. The customer's attitude <u>exasperated</u> the clerk. _____

14. The <u>exasperated</u> clerk glared at the customer. _____

15. "May I return this radio to the <u>store</u> next week?" asked the customer. _____

16. "I'm sorry," replied the clerk, "but the <u>store</u> policy does not permit returns." _____

17. "<u>That</u> policy is ridiculous!" exclaimed the customer. _____

18. "Well, I can't do anything about <u>that</u>," sighed the clerk. _____

19. "May I make a <u>complaint</u> about the policy?" asked the customer. _____

20. "Yes, please write it on that form and put it in the <u>complaint</u> box," said the clerk. _____

Adverbs

An **adverb** modifies a verb, an adjective, or another adverb. An adverb tells *how, when, where,* or *to what extent*.
Examples:

Our skates moved *effortlessly*. (tells how)
The ice is glistening *now*. (tells when)
The canals are frozen *there*. (tells where)
The air was *very* dry. (tells to what extent)

DIRECTIONS ▷ Underline the adverb or adverbs in each sentence. Then write the word that each adverb modifies and write *verb, adjective,* or *adverb* to identify the modified word.

1. High on the mesas of Arizona live the Hopi Indians. _____

2. Despite the harshness of their environment, the Hopis have clung very tenaciously to their way of life. _____

3. The Hopi religion kept them free from outside influences and helped them maintain their extremely interesting culture. _____

4. Tourists frequently visit Hopi villages to learn about sacred Hopi ceremonies. _____

5. The Snake Dance is the most famous of these ceremonies. _____

6. Hopi rituals are based entirely on the need for water to maintain life. _____

7. Never are visitors allowed to participate in these rituals. _____

8. The Hopi use brightly colored dolls called "kachinas" to represent the spirit world. _____

9. Kachina dolls are carved from cottonwood root that has been thoroughly dried. _____

10. Carving these kachina dolls is an unusually painstaking process. _____

11. Now some of these kachina dolls are made for sale. _____

DIRECTIONS ▷ Write an adverb that is most nearly opposite in meaning to the adverb shown.

12. rapidly _____

13. strongly _____

14. noisily _____

15. roughly _____

Comparisons with Adverbs

Adverbs have three forms of comparison: **positive**, **comparative**, and **superlative**.
The **positive** form of an adverb is used when no comparison is being made.
Example:

The sun will set *early.* Ice formed *quickly* on the windshield.

The **comparative** form is used to compare two actions. Form the comparative of most short adverbs by adding *er* to the positive form. With other adverbs, use *more* or *less.*
Examples:

Sunset comes *earlier* in the winter than in the summer.

Weather changes *more quickly* in winter than in fall.

The **superlative** form is used to compare three or more actions. Form the superlative of most short adverbs by adding *est* to the positive form. With other adverbs, use *most* or *least.*
Examples:

Sunset comes *earliest* of all at the winter solstice.

Weather changes *most quickly* with an east wind.

Some adverbs have irregular comparative and superlative forms. Use *farther* and *farthest* to compare distances. Use *further* and *furthest* to compare quantity, time, or degree.
Examples:

far, farther, farthest   far, further, furthest

DIRECTIONS ▷ Write *farther, farthest, further,* or *furthest* to complete each sentence.

1. Sea tortoises can swim _____ than seals can.

2. The oceanographic institute will provide _____ information on the sea tortoise.

3. The gray whale can swim _____ of all without growing tired.

4. Scientists think the albatross can fly _____ than any other bird without roosting.

5. The _____ one reads about these animals, the grander their stamina and resourcefulness appear.

DIRECTIONS ▷ Write the correct form of the adverb in parentheses.

6. Two eagles are soaring _____ above the cliffs.
   (high)

7. Of all North American birds, the eagle flies _____.
   (high)

8. In the jungle an animal must move _____ to remain safe.
   (stealthily)

9. The animal that moves _____ of all will be safe and well fed.
   (stealthily)

10. A mongoose can move _____ than a snake.
    (stealthily)

11. The cheetah runs _____ of all jungle animals.
    (swiftly)

Negatives

Negatives are words that mean "no." The words *no, not, never, nowhere, nothing, nobody, no one, neither, scarcely,* and *barely* are common negatives. Use only one negative in a sentence.

Examples:

      CORRECT *No one* should *ever* drive on ice.

      INCORRECT *No one* should *never* drive on ice.

DIRECTIONS ▷ Underline the negative word in each sentence.

1. Hugh barely made it to practice on time.

2. The coach never allowed you to play if you were late more than twice.

3. Hugh couldn't afford to miss another game.

4. It wasn't easy making the team in the first place.

5. That day, Hugh could scarcely clear the hurdles.

6. Hugh did not want the coach to remember his poor performance at the tryouts.

DIRECTIONS ▷ Underline the word in parentheses that correctly completes the sentence. Avoid double negatives.

7. Haven't you (never, ever) eaten fish?

8. There isn't (no, any) tastier food, I think.

9. You won't (never, ever) find shellfish along the surface of the sea.

10. There is (no, any) way they can move there.

11. Shellfish haven't (any, no) means of movement except along the sea bottom.

12. Some people won't (ever, never) eat lobster or crab meat.

13. Marvin said that he had (ever, never) eaten mackerel before.

14. He says nothing (ever, never) tasted so good.

15. When you live near the sea, buying fresh fish is (no, any) problem at all.

16. There isn't (anywhere, nowhere) better for someone who likes fish.

Adverb or Adjective?

Some words can be used as either adverbs or adjectives.
Words that modify nouns or pronouns can only be adjectives (real, good, bad, sure).
Examples:
> I am *sure* we are on time. This food is not *good*. The lemon is *bad*.

Some words can only be adverbs (really, badly, surely, almost).
Examples:
> The food is *really* good. I felt *badly* last night. It is *almost* time to go to bed.

DIRECTIONS ▷ **Write *adverb* or *adjective* to identify the underlined word in each sentence.**

1. Nicole arrived at the parade grounds <u>early</u>. _____

2. As usual, her dog was behaving <u>badly</u>. _____

3. Nicole hoped obedience school would make a <u>good</u> dog out of Bandit. _____

4. She and Bandit practiced <u>slow</u> figure eights around the field. _____

5. As Bandit pulled at his leash, Nicole began to feel <u>most</u> annoyed. _____

6. They were <u>sure</u> to fail miserably at this exercise. _____

7. Bandit <u>really</u> was a mischievous dog. _____

8. Getting Bandit to behave will be a <u>real</u> achievement. _____

9. Hyenas have <u>really</u> strong jaws. _____

10. In hyena society, the top-ranking female <u>almost</u> always leads the pack. _____

DIRECTIONS ▷ **Underline the correct word in parentheses.**

11. (Most, Almost) any dog can enter obedience school.

12. Even a dog that behaves (badly, bad) can be trained.

13. Dogs older than six months can do (good, well) in obedience training.

14. A young puppy is (really, real) not able to remember commands.

15. A (good, well) command is one that is given clearly and firmly.

DIRECTIONS ▷ **Write a short paragraph describing something your pet or a friend's pet has done. Use at last four of the adverbs and adjectives on this page correctly.**

_____

_____

_____

_____

_____

Prepositions and Prepositional Phrases

A **preposition** shows the relationship of a noun or pronoun to another word in the sentence. Common prepositions are *about, along, among, beneath, with, before, behind, in, at, during, for, from, on, by, through, of, off, until, into, to, under, between,* and *over*.
Example:
> I walked *along* the beach.

The noun or pronoun that follows a preposition is the **object of the preposition**.
Example:
> The sands *of* the *beach* were white.

A **prepositional phrase** is made up of a preposition, the object of the preposition, and all the words in between.
Examples:
> Who lives *in that house*? It is supported *by wooden stilts*.

DIRECTIONS ▷ Underline each prepositional phrase in the sentences. Circle each preposition.

1. Karl grabbed the seat by the window.
2. Then he ran his fingers through his hair and arranged his pencils in neat rows across his desk.
3. He knew he was ready for the test.
4. He had been studying since Saturday afternoon.
5. Still, when his teacher distributed the test sheets, Karl felt his heart pound against his shirt.
6. "Don't panic," he muttered to himself. "You're lost without confidence and concentration."
7. Karl looked out the smudged window with a long face.
8. Finally, with a sigh, he focused his thoughts on the first test question and started working.
9. The boat took us into deep water.
10. We stopped in a certain place.
11. Everyone scanned the water through binoculars.
12. One of the passengers saw the tail of a whale.
13. All heads turned to the right.
14. We could see eight whales in the group.
15. We felt the excitement of the moment.
16. Most whales are among the endangered species.
17. Concern for the world's whales is growing.
18. The ship steamed slowly down the river.
19. Many passengers leaned over the railing.
20. The ship was bound for England.
21. People waved to the passengers.

Prepositions and Prepositional Phrases, page 2

DIRECTIONS ▷ Underline each prepositional phrase in the sentences. Circle each preposition.

1. A few people walked down the gangplank.
2. The ship would soon be sailing into the Atlantic Ocean.
3. The trip would last for five days.
4. For many people, this had been their first sea voyage.
5. That must have been a pleasant form of travel.
6. The Chinese were the greatest sailors in history.
7. The rudder, the single mast, the square sail, and the compass were all invented by the Chinese.
8. Can you imagine steering a boat without a rudder?
9. Sailors have always been guided by the stars in clear weather.
10. The use of the compass made navigation in cloudy weather possible.
11. The compass was first mentioned in a book written in 1117.
12. The compass was actually invented in China at a much earlier date.
13. The time of this invention was the fourth century B.C.
14. Last year the students in our school worked with the local museum.
15. It was an exciting project for everyone.
16. At the museum's invitation, students created their own art exhibition.
17. The theme for the exhibition was "Assignment 1890s: Students Look at America."
18. The head of our social studies department divided students into groups.
19. One group studied changes in transportation during the 1890s.
20. Another group studied the lives of children in the late nineteenth century.
21. Still another group of students concentrated on the growing interest in photography.
22. The 1890s was an important period for the arts in America.
23. Students designed an exhibit for each major theme in the show.
24. One exhibit was about the world's fair held in Chicago in 1893.
25. Two students made a model of the great Ferris wheel built by George W. Gale Ferris.
26. It was one of the attractions at the fair.
27. People came to Chicago from many countries.
28. The fair was a highlight of the 1890s.
29. In the late nineteenth century, the market for children's toys boomed.
30. Small children built objects with alphabet blocks.

Prepositional Phrases Used as Adjectives or Adverbs

> A prepositional phrase that modifies, or describes, a noun or a pronoun is an **adjective phrase**. An adjective phrase tells *what kind, which one,* or *how many.*
>
> *Examples:*
>
> The killer whale is a species *of porpoise.* (tells what kind)
>
> That whale *with the unusual markings* is our favorite. (tells which one)
>
> A pod *of twenty whales* was sighted recently. (tells how many)
>
> A prepositional phrase that modifies a verb, an adjective, or an adverb is an **adverb phrase**. An adverb phrase tells *how, when, where,* or *how often.*
>
> *Examples:*
>
> The porpoises performed *with ease.* (tells how)
>
> Shows begin *on the hour.* (tells when)
>
> The porpoises swim *in a large tank.* (tells where)
>
> They are rewarded *after each trick.* (tells how often)

DIRECTIONS Read each sentence and write the prepositional phrase. Write *adjective phrase* or *adverb phrase* to identify its use. Then write the word or phrase the prepositional phrase modifies.

1. That coral reef may have been growing for a thousand years.

   _____

2. Coral near the water's surface is beautiful but very fragile.

   _____

3. Sand that settles on live coral can suffocate and kill it.

   _____

4. Many coral formations are destroyed by ignorant or irresponsible divers.

   _____

5. Most damage to a coral reef, however, is caused accidentally.

   _____

6. Scuba divers should never brush against coral formations.

   _____

7. Underwater photographers should not lie or sit on the coral.

   _____

8. No photograph is worth the cost of dead or damaged coral.

   _____

9. Underwater guides at many popular diving destinations are educating new and experienced divers alike.

   _____

10. They know they must preserve these precious resources under the sea.

   _____

Prepositional Phrases Used as Adjectives or Adverbs, page 2

 **DIRECTIONS** Read each sentence and write the prepositional phrase. Write *adjective phrase* or *adverb phrase* to identify its use. Then write the word or phrase the prepositional phrase modifies.

1. The migrations of birds are remarkable events in nature.

   _____

2. Many species of migrating birds cover thousands of miles each year.

   _____

3. The journey of the Arctic tern may be the longest.

   _____

4. Every autumn this bird flies from the far North to Antarctica.

   _____

5. The route covers a distance of approximately 9,000 miles.

   _____

6. Many birds migrate at night, and they travel for long distances across the open ocean.

   _____

7. How do they find their way to their destinations?

   _____

8. Scientists have interesting theories about bird navigation.

   _____

9. Some experts think that birds are sensitive to the earth's magnetic field.

   _____

10. Apparently birds use stars for reference points in their long flights.

    _____

11. One reason for the birds' migration is their need for food.

    _____

12. When winter begins in northern climates, food becomes scarce for many species.

    _____

13. Insects are more plentiful in warmer areas.

    _____

14. Many birds fly north in summer so that they can establish nesting territories.

    _____

15. The longer summertime days in northern latitudes are an advantage for birds that are feeding and raising their young.

    _____

Using Prepositions Correctly

Use **between** for two and **among** for three or more.
Examples:
> I divided the oranges *between* Myra and Sarah. I divided the oranges *among* Myra, Sarah, and Jan.

Use **at** to mean "in the location of." Use **to** to mean "in a direction toward."
Examples:
> The picnic is *at* the lake. Let's go *to* the lake.

Use **beside** to mean "next to, at the side of." Use **besides** to mean "in addition."
Examples:
> My car was parked *beside* your car. *Besides* getting my teeth cleaned, I had a cavity filled.

Use **in** to mean "already inside." Use **into** to tell about movement from the outside to the inside.
Examples:
> He is *in* the house. I am going *into* the house.

DIRECTIONS ▷ **Each sentence contains one error. Rewrite the sentence correctly.**

1. Lupe visited her aunt into Guatemala.

_____

2. Beside wanting to see a new country, Lupe wanted her aunt to teach her how to weave.

_____

3. Lupe's aunt was between the best weavers in her town.

_____

4. Lupe knew her training in her aunt's would require much work.

_____

5. Lupe's first trip in town from her aunt's country house was overwhelming.

_____

6. Artisans displaying their wares crowded besides food stalls and animal vendors.

_____

7. She couldn't believe so much could be happening into one place.

_____

8. After Lupe had been to the market some time, she became hungry.

_____

9. She stood among two food stalls, trying to decide what to buy to eat.

_____

10. Lupe remembered she had several juice drinks into her backpack.

_____

Four Kinds of Sentences

A **sentence** is a group of words that expresses a complete thought and has a subject and a predicate. Begin a sentence with a capital letter, and end it with a punctuation mark.
A **declarative sentence** makes a statement. Use a period at the end of a declarative sentence.
Example:

      Janelle is painting a picture of an imaginary place.

An **interrogative sentence** asks a question. Use a question mark at the end of an interrogative sentence.
Example:

      Did she dream it up by herself?

An **imperative sentence** gives a command or makes a request. Use a period at the end of an imperative sentence. Remember that the subject of imperative sentences is always <u>you</u>. However, the subject is "understood" and therefore does not appear in the sentence.
Example:

      Think about all the uses for artwork.

An **exclamatory sentence** expresses strong feeling. Use an exclamation point at the end of an exclamatory sentence.
Example:

      What fantastic places those are!

DIRECTIONS Read each group of words. Write *sentence* or *not a sentence* to identify each group of words.

1. What fun it is to watch a mime perform! _____

2. Notice the mime's white makeup. _____

3. The funny, jerky movements of the mime's performance. _____

4. Have you ever seen one at a fair or carnival? _____

5. I have. _____

6. María has been telling Hakim an amazing story. _____

7. It is *Fantastic Voyage*, a movie. _____

8. To save a dying man. _____

9. Scientists are shrunk to microscopic size. _____

10. A tiny submarine. _____

11. Into a world of unimagined complexity and beauty. _____

12. Dangers await these brave voyagers. _____

13. Through the valves of a beating heart. _____

14. Fortunately, the operation was a complete success. _____

15. At the last minute, through the patient's tear duct. _____

Four Kinds of Sentences, page 2

DIRECTIONS ▷ Add the correct punctuation mark at the end of each sentence. Then write whether each sentence is *declarative, interrogative, exclamatory,* or *imperative.*

1. Have you ever wondered about life in a swamp _____

2. What a paradise swamps are for plant life _____

3. Think about the beautiful water hyacinth _____

4. Do you know why this plant never gets waterlogged _____

5. The water hyacinth has a waxy skin _____

6. How amazing those mangrove trees are _____

7. Can they actually grow in salt water _____

8. Look carefully at the next-to-lowest branch on the right _____

9. Do you see the iguana sunbathing _____

10. How incredible its camouflage is _____

DIRECTIONS ▷ Write each sentence correctly.

11. if you ever get a chance, stop and watch a mime

_____

12. they like to imitate you behind your back

_____

13. my goodness, there's one now

_____

14. fiddler crabs appear at low tide

_____

15. look at the pincers on the male crabs

_____

16. how unusual they are

_____

17. can you see why they are called fiddler crabs

_____

18. what do they use the pincers for

_____

19. the crabs use them to signal to females and to protect their territory

_____

20. they are small, but they look very fierce

_____

49

Complete and Simple Subjects

Every sentence is made up of two parts, a subject and a predicate.
The **complete subject** includes all the words that tell whom or what the sentence is about.
Example:
> My two older *brothers* stared at me silently.

The **simple subject** is the main word or words in the complete subject. Sometimes the complete subject and the simple subject are the same.
Examples:
> My two older *brothers* stared at me silently. *I* blinked.

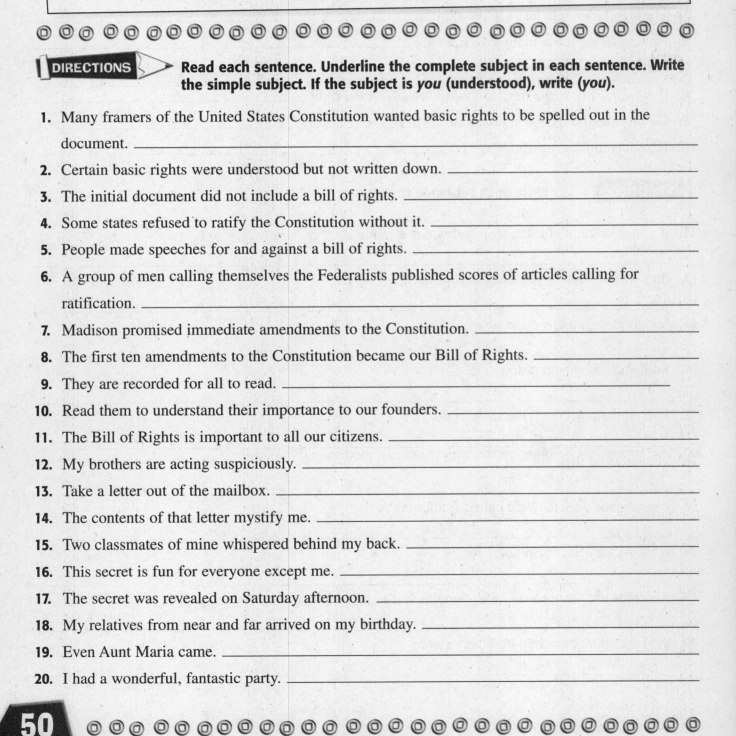

DIRECTIONS ➤ Read each sentence. Underline the complete subject in each sentence. Write the simple subject. If the subject is *you* (understood), write (*you*).

1. Many framers of the United States Constitution wanted basic rights to be spelled out in the document. _____

2. Certain basic rights were understood but not written down. _____

3. The initial document did not include a bill of rights. _____

4. Some states refused to ratify the Constitution without it. _____

5. People made speeches for and against a bill of rights. _____

6. A group of men calling themselves the Federalists published scores of articles calling for ratification. _____

7. Madison promised immediate amendments to the Constitution. _____

8. The first ten amendments to the Constitution became our Bill of Rights. _____

9. They are recorded for all to read. _____

10. Read them to understand their importance to our founders. _____

11. The Bill of Rights is important to all our citizens. _____

12. My brothers are acting suspiciously. _____

13. Take a letter out of the mailbox. _____

14. The contents of that letter mystify me. _____

15. Two classmates of mine whispered behind my back. _____

16. This secret is fun for everyone except me. _____

17. The secret was revealed on Saturday afternoon. _____

18. My relatives from near and far arrived on my birthday. _____

19. Even Aunt Maria came. _____

20. I had a wonderful, fantastic party. _____

Complete and Simple Predicates

The **complete predicate** includes all the words in the predicate.
Examples:
My two older brothers *stared at me silently.* I *blinked.*
The **simple predicate** is the main verb or verbs in the complete predicate. Sometimes the complete predicate and the simple predicate are the same.
Examples:
My two older brothers *stared* at me silently. I *blinked.*

DIRECTIONS ▷ Underline the complete predicate of each sentence. Write the simple predicate in each complete predicate.

1. Amanda invited six girls to an unusual birthday party. _____

2. All the girls met at a stable in the desert. _____

3. Amanda's Grandma Jean had rented eight horses, one for each girl and one for herself.

_____

4. Lunches and canteens had been packed into each of the eight saddle bags. _____

5. The girls were given the most docile horses. _____

6. None of the girls had any real trouble getting to the lunch spot. _____

7. The girls returned to the stable after a brief rest and an investigation of the desert landscape.

_____

8. Australia's largest city is Sydney. _____

9. Sydney is a major port in southeastern Australia. _____

10. Australia's leading exports pass through the port. _____

11. These include wool, wheat, and meat. _____

12. The harbor is spectacular. _____

13. One prominent building on the waterfront is a modern opera house. _____

14. The Sydney Harbor Bridge spans Port Jackson gracefully with a single steel arch. _____

15. Bondi Beach on the Pacific Ocean is a popular recreation area. _____

16. Visitors at Taronga Zoological Gardens admire Australia's unusual animals. _____

17. The first sight of a koala delights most viewers. _____

18. The platypus is one of Australia's most unusual animals. _____

19. You have probably seen pictures of koalas and kangaroos. _____

20. Many Australian plants and animals are found nowhere else in the world. _____

Compound Subjects and Compound Predicates

A **compound subject** consists of two or more subjects that have the same predicate. The simple subjects in a compound subject are usually joined by *and* or *or*. If there are three or more simple subjects in a compound subject, use commas to separate them.
Examples:
> The *craters* and *plains* of the moon have had no human visitors.
> *Darryl*, *Setsu*, and *I* will present a report about that mission.

A **compound predicate** consists of two or more predicates that have the same subject. The simple predicates in a compound predicate are usually joined by *and* or *or*. If there are three or more simple predicates in a compound predicate, use commas to separate them.
Examples:
> We *will find* the card catalog or *will ask* the librarian for help.
> The three of us *whispered, pointed,* and *made* notes.

> **DIRECTIONS** Add a compound subject or a compound predicate to each group of words to make a complete sentence.

1. are two beautiful Olympic sports. _____

_____

2. The United States and the Soviet Union _____

_____

3. are worn by Olympic champions. _____

_____

4. Olympic competitors _____

_____

5. In the 1980s Seoul, Los Angeles, and Moscow _____

_____

6. have astonished people with their talents. _____

_____

7. Every aspiring athlete _____

_____

8. have inspired young athletes throughout the world. _____

_____

9. The dream of winning an Olympic medal _____

_____

10. Friends, parents, and coaches _____

_____

Compound Subjects and Compound Predicates, page 2

DIRECTIONS Tell whether each sentence has a compound subject or a compound predicate. Then write the simple subject in each compound subject and the simple predicate in each compound predicate.

1. Ms. Ramírez and Mr. Singh play in a local orchestra. _____

2. The orchestra gives concerts and also donates its services for charity events. _____

3. Ms. Ramírez manages the woodwind section and plays the oboe. _____

4. Mr. Singh plays the violin and acts as the concertmaster. _____

5. Ms. Johnston plans the schedule and conducts the orchestra. _____

6. The musicians and the ushers are volunteers. _____

7. The musicians gather at the theater every Thursday night and practice. _____

8. Audiences clap and cheer after every performance. _____

9. Either a symphony or a concerto is generally on the program. _____

10. The orchestra has toured our state and has appeared in several major cities. _____

11. Clarinetists, flutists, and oboists play in the woodwind section. _____

12. A harp or a piano may be added to the orchestra for a selection. _____

13. Percussion instruments such as drums vary and enrich the orchestra's sound. _____

14. Felicia and Alfio were unhappy. _____

15. Alfio came out of the house and joined Felicia. _____

16. The young girl and her twin brother would have a birthday soon. _____

17. They enjoyed life on the farm but were somewhat lonely. _____

18. Their mother and father had said nothing about the twins' birthday. _____

19. Alfio and Felicia had not expressed anything directly to their parents. _____

20. The twins' parents understood the problem and had discussed it. _____

21. The children's friends lived several miles away and rarely visited. _____

22. Felicia's parents sometimes talked with each other but kept their voices soft. _____

23. Felicia and Alfio woke up early on the morning of their birthday. _____

24. They rushed down the stairs and ran into the kitchen. _____

25. Mother was fixing breakfast and wished them a happy birthday. _____

Simple and Compound Sentences

A **simple sentence** expresses only one complete thought.
Example:
> Objects from space fall into the atmosphere.

A **compound sentence** is made up of two or more simple sentences. The simple sentences usually are joined by a comma and a coordinating conjunction—which is a connecting word such as *and, or,* or *but*—or by a semicolon.
Examples:
> Friction makes meteors incredibly hot, *and* they burn up miles above the earth's surface.
> Some large meteors do not burn up completely; they are called meteorites.

DIRECTIONS ▷ **Use a combining word or a semicolon to combine each pair of sentences into one compound sentence.**

1. Bicycles and feet take you in and out of small hamlets. They put you in contact with everyday life.

_____

_____

2. People living in the countryside see fewer tourists. They are often eager to talk to foreigners.

_____

_____

3. You may be able to learn the local language. Some of the local people may speak English.

_____

_____

4. Denzel's father agreed to help him. The two of them took a drive on a calm, sunny day.

_____

_____

5. Denzel held his wind gauge upright outside the car window. The open notch on the gauge faced into the wind.

_____

_____

6. The air entered the wind gauge. The pressure lifted the plastic foam ball.

_____

_____

7. Denzel's father told him the car's speed. Denzel marked it on the cardboard.

_____

_____

Simple and Compound Sentences, page 2

 **DIRECTIONS** Underline each simple subject once and underline each verb twice. Then identify the sentence by writing *simple* or *compound*.

1. Traveling by train may be an easy way to get around Europe, but it is not the best way.

   _____

2. Have you ever considered bicycling or walking? _____

3. Trains take you in and out of big cities and either speed you through villages or bypass them

   altogether. _____

4. Travelers to big cities often experience only the more negative aspects of a country. _____

5. Have you seen the Meteor Crater in Arizona? _____

6. This huge hole measures about 4,150 feet across and about 570 feet deep. _____

7. A meteorite crashed there perhaps 50,000 years ago, or it may have fallen even earlier.

   _____

8. In 1908, a meteorite streaked across the Siberian sky; people could see it for hundreds of miles.

   _____

9. Did it really weigh hundreds of tons? _____

10. In 1947, another meteorite exploded over Siberia; it created more than 200 craters. _____

11. Denzel was interested in weather forecasting; he decided to make a wind gauge for his science

    project. _____

12. Denzel made his wind gauge from a plastic drinking straw, two small pieces of plastic foam, two

    pins, some tape, and a piece of cardboard. _____

13. First he made a plastic foam ball smaller than the opening of the straw. _____

14. He cut a notch in the straw about a half inch from one end, and then he plugged that end of the

    straw with a small piece of plastic foam. _____

15. Next, Denzel cut a small hole in the side of the straw near the other end. _____

16. Denzel put the straw on the center of the cardboard with the notch facing forward; he pinned the

    lower end of the straw to the cardboard just above the notch. _____

17. He dropped the little plastic foam ball into the top end of the straw, and then he pinned this end

    just below the small hole. _____

18. Denzel held the straw in place on the cardboard with some strips of tape. _____

19. He had finished making the wind gauge, but he needed to calibrate it. _____

20. Denzel had an idea, and he asked his parents for help. _____

Conjunctions

A **conjunction** is a word used to join words or groups of words. Some commonly used conjunctions are *although, and, as, because, but, for, however, if, nor, or, since, than, that, though, unless, when, whereas, whether, while,* and *yet.*
Example:
>   Carissa *and* I drove to the school.

A **coordinating conjunction** is a word used to join words that have the same function in a sentence. *And, but,* and *or* are coordinating conjunctions.
Examples:
>   Metal *or* stone cabinets are uncommon. (joins two subjects)
>   Crabs are small, *but* they look very fierce. (joins two sentences)

Correlative conjunctions are pairs of words that join individual words, groups of words, or sentences. Some commonly used pairs are *either...or, neither...nor, not only...but also, both...and,* and *just...so.*
Example:
>   The class was *not only* long *but also* boring.

DIRECTIONS ▷ Underline the conjunctions in each sentence. Then identify each one by writing *coordinating* or *correlative.*

1. Both windsurfing and sailing can be exciting sports. _____

2. Windsurfers and sailboats use sails for moving across the water. _____

3. Windsurfing is fun, but many people consider it more difficult than sailing. _____

4. Windsurfing requires both strength and balance. _____

5. A windsurfer must balance on a narrow board while holding on to the sail, but a sailor can sit inside the craft while steering. _____

6. Either windsurfing or sailing, however, requires skill. _____

7. Just as the sailor requires knowledge of wind dynamics, so must the windsurfer understand how balance controls movement. _____

8. It would be fun to ride to the island, but not on a windsurfer. _____

9. Carmen does not go windsurfing or sailing. _____

DIRECTIONS ▷ Write a short paragraph about an active sport you like. Use coordinating and correlative conjunctions in your paragraph.

_____

_____

_____

_____

Interjections

An **interjection** is a word or a group of words that expresses strong feeling. Some commonly used interjections are *Wow!, Aha!, Hooray!, Of course!, Oh, no!,* and *Yikes!* You can separate an interjection from the rest of a sentence with either an exclamation point or a comma.
Examples:

Hey, is that your painting?   Wow! That's really amazing!

DIRECTIONS ▷ **Write an interjection to complete each sentence.**

1. _____! I think we're locked out of the house.

2. _____, we're just going to have to find another way to get in.

3. _____, the only way I know is through the upstairs bedroom.

4. _____! Do you mean we have to climb that tree to get there?

5. _____! Do you want everyone in the neighborhood to hear us?

6. _____! That branch scratched me.

7. _____, watch out for that wasp nest.

8. _____! I hate bugs.

9. _____! I didn't think you could do it.

10. _____! We made it!

DIRECTIONS ▷ **Write each sentence. Insert the correct punctuation mark after each interjection.**

11. Hey Who do you think could have left that shoe here?

_____

12. Oh just ask Kim; she's the school detective.

_____

13. Ah this will be an easy case to solve.

_____

14. Impossible How can you tell whose shoe this is?

_____

15. Well do you notice that the shoelaces are green?

_____

16. Gee doesn't Mark wear sneakers with green laces?

_____

Avoiding Sentence Fragments and Run-on Sentences

Avoid using **sentence fragments**, which lack either a subject or a verb and do not express a complete thought.
Examples:
> INCORRECT: Alvin's birthday next Saturday.
> CORRECT: Alvin's birthday is next Saturday.

A **run-on sentence** results when two or more simple sentences are combined without the proper punctuation to separate them.
Examples:
> INCORRECT: A crater can be formed by a bomb it can be formed by a meteorite.
> CORRECT: A crater can be formed by a bomb, or it can be formed by a meteorite.

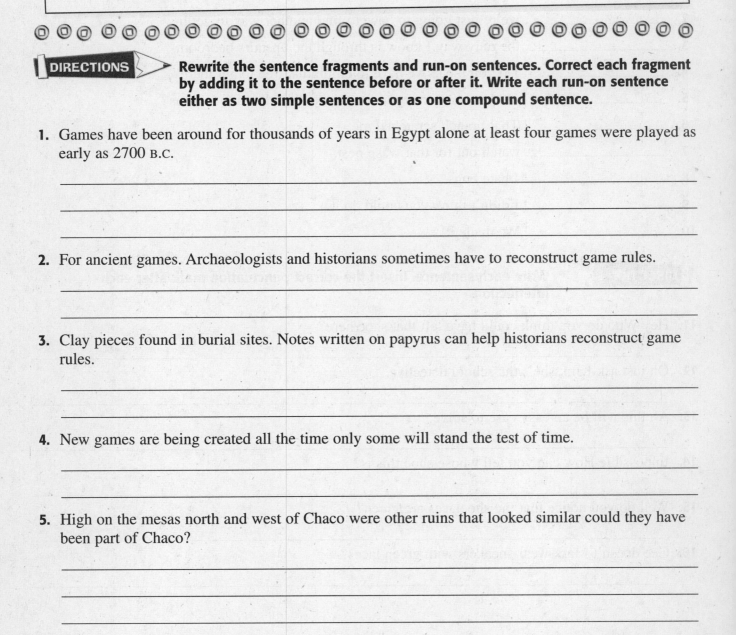

| DIRECTIONS | Rewrite the sentence fragments and run-on sentences. Correct each fragment by adding it to the sentence before or after it. Write each run-on sentence either as two simple sentences or as one compound sentence.

1. Games have been around for thousands of years in Egypt alone at least four games were played as early as 2700 B.C.

   _____

   _____

2. For ancient games. Archaeologists and historians sometimes have to reconstruct game rules.

   _____

   _____

3. Clay pieces found in burial sites. Notes written on papyrus can help historians reconstruct game rules.

   _____

   _____

4. New games are being created all the time only some will stand the test of time.

   _____

   _____

5. High on the mesas north and west of Chaco were other ruins that looked similar could they have been part of Chaco?

   _____

   _____

   _____

Avoiding Sentence Fragments and Run-on Sentences, page 2

| DIRECTIONS > **Rewrite the scene, correcting sentence fragments and eliminating run-ons.**

MANDY: Who wouldn't? Want to go to the end-of-the-year party?

SARA: Jeffrey doesn't. If they aren't going to have live music.

MANDY: What does that matter I suppose hearing live music is the only thing that matters?

SARA: It is to some people it is to Jeff and his best friend, Mike.

MANDY: Who cares? What they think? They wouldn't know good music if their lives depended on it.

SARA: I know I can't believe that would actually stop them from going.

MANDY: Well. The party will be much more fun without them. If they are going to make such a fuss.

SARA: You're right but they are such fun Jessica thinks the party will be boring without them.

MANDY: I have an idea why not let Jeff and Mike act as disc jockeys that way they can play the music most people like.

SARA: Wow, that is. A great idea!

Combining Sentences to Avoid Choppy Writing

Avoid the continuous use of short, choppy sentences. Combine choppy sentences by using appositives, compound subjects, or compound predicates.
Example:

(CHOPPY SENTENCES) Madagascar is the world's fourth-largest island. It lies off the coast of Africa in the Indian Ocean.

(COMBINED BY FORMING AN APPOSITIVE) Madagascar, the world's fourth-largest island, lies off the coast of Africa in the Indian Ocean.

DIRECTIONS **Combine each set of sentences. Follow the directions in parentheses. Remember to use the proper punctuation in your new sentences.**

1. Mr. Escudero was a strong supporter of public television. He decided to have his eighth-grade class debate the merits of TV. (Form an appositive.)

_____

_____

2. He divided the class into pro-TV and anti-TV factions. He supplied the students with research materials. (Form a compound predicate.)

_____

_____

3. The students searched books and magazines for supporting facts. They organized their arguments. (Form a compound predicate.)

_____

_____

4. Mr. Escudero began to believe that they should have limited the scope of the debate to commercial TV. Some of the students also believed that the scope should have been limited to commercial TV. (Form a compound subject.)

_____

_____

_____

5. Some of the books pointed out the differences in programming between commercial and public TV. Some of the magazines pointed out the same differences. (Form a compound subject.)

_____

_____

6. Portuguese explorers were the first Europeans to see Madagascar. They landed there around 1500. (Form an appositive.)

_____

_____

Complex Sentences

A **complex sentence** has an independent clause and one or more subordinate, or dependent, clauses. Subordinate clauses often tell *why, when, where, what,* or *which one.*
An **independent clause** expresses a complete thought and can stand alone as a simple sentence.
Examples:
> Some pollution affects our homes and schools.
> If their neighbors cooperate, *young people and adults can clean up their neighborhoods.*

A **subordinate clause** contains a subject and a predicate, but it does not express a complete thought, and it cannot stand alone. A subordinate clause often begins with a subordinating conjunction, such as *after, although, because, before, if, since, when,* or *while.*
Examples:
> People became more sensitive to pollution problems *after they learned about toxic waste.*
> If we want pollution-free neighborhoods, shouldn't we work together?

DIRECTIONS ▷ Write *independent* or *subordinate* to identify each clause.

1. fossils are found imbedded in rock

2. scientists dissolve the rock over a screen

3. when the rock falls through the screen

4. if a fossil is left behind

5. while the rock is dissolving

6. so that we can learn about earlier forms of life

7. unless the workers are extremely careful

8. the fossil may be destroyed

9. because the discoveries can be so fascinating

10. before they report their findings

11. if you go to New York City

12. since they were pollution fighters

13. they called themselves the Toxic Avengers

14. although it was located next to a school

15. the Toxic Avengers planned a response

16. when a crowd gathered for a public rally

17. after the rally was held

18. consider a visit to Brooklyn

19. fifteen teenagers there gained some fame

20. because public awareness grew

Complex Sentences, page 2

 **DIRECTIONS** Rewrite each sentence. Add a subordinate clause beginning with the subordinating conjunction in parentheses. Remember that a subordinate clause contains a subject and a verb.

1. Scientists may discover fossils. (while)

_____

_____

2. You can see some unusual fossil bones. (if)

_____

_____

3. No one there should touch the fossils. (because)

_____

_____

4. Volunteer firefighters respond. (when)

_____

_____

5. They need special training. (since)

_____

_____

6. They often must work. (where)

_____

_____

7. Volunteer firefighters get my vote of thanks. (because)

_____

_____

8. The chief directed the firefighters. (as)

_____

_____

9. Most of us cheered and waved. (when)

_____

_____

10. All of us worried about the firefighters' safety. (although)

_____

_____

Adjective Clauses

An **adjective clause** modifies a noun or a pronoun. The majority of adjective clauses are introduced by relative pronouns such as *who, whose, whom, which,* and *that*.
Examples:
> She lost the ring *that you gave her*. The women *who work in the office* are well paid.

An adjective clause can be restrictive or nonrestrictive. A **restrictive clause** is one that points out what person or thing is meant: that is, it restricts the statement to that person or thing. It cannot be omitted without changing the meaning of the sentence.
Example:
> The person *who received the most votes* was elected.

A **nonrestrictive** clause is descriptive or explanatory and can be omitted without changing the essential meaning. The person or thing that is spoken of is definitely indicated without the clause.
Example:
> My father, *who was coaching the baseball team,* met us at the ballpark.

A restrictive clause is not punctuated; a nonrestrictive clause is set off with commas.

◎ ◎◎ ◎◎◎ ◎◎◎◎◎◎◎◎ ◎◎◎◎◎◎◎◎◎◎◎◎ ◎◎◎◎◎◎◎◎◎◎◎ ◎◎◎ ◎

DIRECTIONS Underline the adjective clause in each sentence once. Underline the relative pronoun twice. Then write *restrictive* or *nonrestrictive* to identify which kind of adjective clause it is.

1. Alberta Hunter, who was a famous singer, began her career when she was only twelve years old. _____

2. She sang in clubs that featured blues and jazz bands. _____

3. She later sang at a Beale Street club that was known as the home of the blues. _____

4. Alberta met Louis Armstrong and Bessie Smith, who were other well-known performers. _____

5. Louis Armstrong is a performer whose music never goes out of style. _____

6. Later in life, Alberta had another career that she enjoyed. _____

7. Nursing was an endeavor that gave her much satisfaction. _____

8. At the age of eighty-two, which was still young for Alberta Hunter, she began entertaining audiences again with her special brand of jazz. _____

DIRECTIONS Write each sentence. Use *which* or *that* to introduce the adjective clause. Add commas where necessary.

9. Jazz is a form of music _____ has many styles.

10. Swing _____ was popularized in the 1940s is a style of jazz.

Adverb Clauses

An **adverb clause** is a subordinate clause that modifies a verb, an adjective, or another adverb. A **subordinating conjunction** introduces an adverb clause. Some common subordinating conjunctions are *when, after, before, since, although,* and *because.* Use commas to set off an adverb clause at the beginning of or in the middle of sentences.
Examples:
Sharon will go *when you are ready.* Mario arrived *before the play began.*

DIRECTIONS **Write the adverb clause from each sentence. Underline the subordinating conjunction in the clause you have written.**

1. Ansel Adams started taking pictures when he was still a teenager.

   _____

2. Although Adams was also an avid conservationist, he is best known for his splendid photographs.

   _____

3. His landscapes look as if they are from another world.

   _____

4. Since Adams died, his photographs have continued to increase in value.

   _____

5. Though many have studied his technique, few have been able to match the clarity of his photographs.

   _____

6. The project was finished because every girl did her share of the work.

   _____

7. While you were at school, I bought groceries and cooked dinner.

   _____

DIRECTIONS **Combine the sentences in each pair, using the subordinating conjunction in parentheses. Add commas where necessary.**

8. Photographing animals is difficult. They are unpredictable. (because)

   _____

9. Keisha used a telephoto lens. She wouldn't startle the heron. (so)

   _____

10. I prefer taking underwater pictures. The water makes photography more challenging. (because)

   _____

   _____

Noun Clauses

A **noun clause** is a subordinate clause used as a noun.
Examples:

> *What you say* is true. (subject)
> She said *that she was a doctor*. (direct object)
> The truth is *that I was not prepared for the test*. (predicate nominative)
> I was frightened *by what I saw*. (object of preposition)

DIRECTIONS Underline the noun clause in each sentence. Write *subject, direct object, predicate nominative,* or *object of a preposition* to show how the noun clause is used.

1. I could tell by the flag on the mailbox that the mail had come. _____

2. Brett found that a letter had come for me. _____

3. What he handed me made me smile. _____

4. The funniest thing about the envelope was that it was made from a brown paper bag. _____

5. I wondered if the sender was very young. _____

6. Brett knew why I thought so. _____

7. Whoever addressed this letter used crayons. _____

8. Brett looked carefully at how it was written. _____

9. When we tore open the envelope, we discovered who had sent it. _____

10. That I had been invited to the party was a pleasant surprise. _____

11. The only remaining question was who else would be there. _____

12. I look forward to talking with whoever comes to that funny party. _____

13. What you say is true. _____

14. Your life is what you make it. _____

15. Charley could see where the rainbow began. _____

DIRECTIONS Add a noun clause to complete each sentence. Remember that a noun clause contains a subject and a verb.

16. _____ will be welcome.

17. You may be surprised by _____.

18. The grand prize will go to _____.

19. _____ will be satisfactory.

20. I had lived near _____.

Participles and Participial Phrases

A **participle** is used as an adjective; that is, it is a form of a verb used as an adjective to modify a noun or a pronoun.
Examples:
> The *running* water was moving dangerously fast.
> The *terrified* horses refused to cross the river.

A **participial phrase** contains a participle and acts as an adjective.
Examples:
> They arrested the man *driving the car*. (present participle)
> The popcorn *drenched with butter* was so delicious. (past participle)

DIRECTIONS ▷ Write the participle or participial phrase from each sentence. Then write the word it modifies.

1. Propelled by dreams of great riches, explorers poured into California.
   _____

2. Pioneers found ideal farming country.
   _____

3. Ranchers staked out miles of grazing land for their cattle and horses.
   _____

4. Flushed with visions of gold-encrusted hills, more adventurers stampeded the state.
   _____

5. Many fights concerning land claims broke out among the gold miners.
   _____

6. Gunfire from battling land-grabbers could often be heard in the hills.
   _____

7. Determined to guard their patches of land, many miners fought to the death.
   _____

8. One map showed the San Joaquin valley as a flowing river of gold.
   _____

9. A new stampede occurred a few decades later when oil, seeping from the earth, was discovered.
   _____

10. Many of these places have become thriving tourist attractions.
    _____

11. Arriving in tour buses, people now photograph these sights.
    _____

12. The student elected by the class made the announcement.
    _____

13. The barking dogs kept us awake all night.
    _____

Gerunds and Gerund Phrases

A **gerund** is a "verb + *ing*" used as a noun.
Examples:

> *Swimming* is good exercise. (subject)
> The girls enjoy *swimming*. (direct object)
> The best exercise is *swimming*. (predicate nominative)
> She was scolded for *swimming*. (object of a preposition)

A **gerund phrase** consists of a gerund and related words.
Example:

> *Swimming in the lake* is good exercise.

 **DIRECTIONS** > Underline the gerund or gerund phrase in each sentence.

1. Although he is famous today, Rudolph Nureyev's birth on a train in Russia was a modest beginning.

2. Nureyev began his great career by dancing with amateur groups.

3. One of his skills was leaping like a gazelle.

4. Leaving Moscow changed Nureyev's career forever.

5. The dance world in London, Paris, and New York competed in praising his performances.

6. At recitals in which Nureyev danced, the orchestra was often drowned out by wild cheering.

7. Watching his impossibly high leaps was an unforgettable experience.

8. His dancing is known to everyone.

9. Driving in a crowded city was a new experience for Nicolás.

10. She could not stop humming that tune.

 **DIRECTIONS** > Write *gerund* or *gerund phrase* to identify the underlined words. Write *subject*, *direct object*, *predicate nominative*, or *object of a preposition* to identify how each gerund or gerund phrase is used in the sentence.

11. <u>Dancing</u> takes many forms. _____

12. Preparation for <u>dancing in a troupe</u> begins early in life. _____

13. <u>Stretching all the muscles</u> takes up much of a dancer's practice time. _____

14. The grandest movement of ballet is <u>leaping</u>. _____

15. In the 1920s modern dancers started <u>moving in a completely new way</u>. _____

16. Now dancers enjoy <u>studying traditional forms</u>. _____

17. The darkness of the night prevented us from <u>finishing the job</u>. _____

18. <u>Rising with the sun</u> did not appeal to him. _____

Infinitives and Infinitive Phrases

An **infinitive** is the present-tense form of a verb preceded by the word *to*. An infinitive may be used as a noun, an adjective, or an adverb.
Examples:
> *To exercise* is a healthful habit. (noun)
> Here is laundry *to wash*. (adjective)
> The choir was ready *to sing*. (adverb)

An **infinitive phrase** consists of an infinitive and the related words that follow it.
Examples:
> Sandra went *to buy groceries.*   Gilbert wanted *to read the book.*

| DIRECTIONS | Write the infinitive or infinitive phrase from each sentence. Then write *noun*, *adjective*, or *adverb* to identify its function in the sentence.

1. People have always sought to protect their rights.

   _____

2. Early Bostonians staged the Boston Tea Party to protest taxation without representation.

   _____

3. To protect their comfortable position, Louis XVI and Marie Antoinette ignored the demands of the French people.

   _____

4. The people of France, weary of going hungry while royalty flourished, were determined to succeed in their revolt.

   _____

5. The creation of a system of public schools established the right of all Americans to become educated.

   _____

6. In the early 1900s, suffragists launched a campaign convincing the country that women should also be allowed to vote.

   _____

7. All the math teachers have papers to grade today.

   _____

8. The angry customer demanded to see the manager.

   _____

9. The rugby team was ready to start.

   _____

| DIRECTIONS | Combine the sentences in each pair by forming an infinitive phrase.

10. Civil libertarians took to the streets and the courts. They wanted to achieve their goal.

    _____

    _____

11. They fought for the rights of all Americans. Now all Americans have voting rights.

    _____

    _____

12. Now each American has a responsibility. Every American must exercise that right to vote.

    _____

Dangling Participles and Split Infinitives

> To correct a **dangling participle**, place the participial phrase closer to the word it modifies.
> *Examples:*
> | INCORRECT | *Playing solitaire*, at the table sat a bored young man. |
> | CORRECT | At the table sat a bored young man *playing solitaire*. |
>
> Avoid **splitting infinitives** with an adverb.
> *Examples:*
> | INCORRECT | I wanted *to slowly see* the city. |
> | CORRECT | I wanted *to see* the city *slowly*. |

 Underline the participial phrase or the infinitive in each sentence. Then write *dangling participle* or *split infinitive* to identify the problem. If the sentence is correct, write *correct*.

1. Raul wanted to desperately gain admission to the writing workshop.

   _____

2. Considering and reconsidering every word, the application form was filled out by Raul.

   _____

3. Raul's next step was to thoughtfully select his best writing samples.

   _____

4. Writing at least two paragraphs every day for the past year, Raul had accumulated many samples.

   _____

5. Hovering over his journal, the decision seemed almost impossible to Raul.

   _____

6. He had expected his best work to somehow leap out from the page.

   _____

7. Shaking his head uncertainly, Raul wondered whether any of his work could be good enough.

   _____

8. He had hoped to actually find at least five outstanding prose selections and two short poems.

   _____

9. Now Raul wondered whether he needed to unfortunately write completely new samples for his application.

   _____

10. Carrying his journal and his application form, Raul asked Mr. Dressler, his English teacher, to advise him.

    _____

11. They told us to speak quickly and to tell the truth.

    _____

12. The boy, hearing the raging river, went to the second story of the house.

    _____

Misplaced Modifiers

Place a **modifier** as close as possible to the word it modifies, or describes.
Examples:

INCORRECT	The man looks like a spy *with the hat*.
CORRECT	The man *with the hat* looks like a spy.

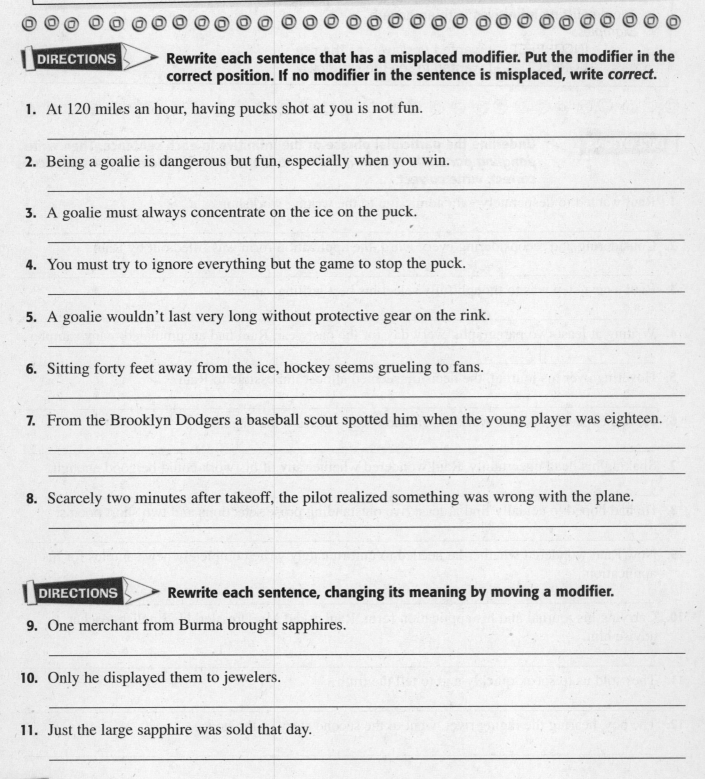

DIRECTIONS ▷ **Rewrite each sentence that has a misplaced modifier. Put the modifier in the correct position. If no modifier in the sentence is misplaced, write *correct*.**

1. At 120 miles an hour, having pucks shot at you is not fun.

2. Being a goalie is dangerous but fun, especially when you win.

3. A goalie must always concentrate on the ice on the puck.

4. You must try to ignore everything but the game to stop the puck.

5. A goalie wouldn't last very long without protective gear on the rink.

6. Sitting forty feet away from the ice, hockey seems grueling to fans.

7. From the Brooklyn Dodgers a baseball scout spotted him when the young player was eighteen.

8. Scarcely two minutes after takeoff, the pilot realized something was wrong with the plane.

DIRECTIONS ▷ **Rewrite each sentence, changing its meaning by moving a modifier.**

9. One merchant from Burma brought sapphires.

10. Only he displayed them to jewelers.

11. Just the large sapphire was sold that day.

Capitalization and End Punctuation in Sentences

Capitalize the first word of a sentence. End a sentence with a period, a question mark, or an exclamation point.
Examples:

My father travels around the country. Has the airplane landed? What amazing places your mind can take you!

 **DIRECTIONS** Circle each letter that should be capitalized. Write the capital letter above it. Then insert needed end punctuation.

1. on our last vacation we went to the desert
2. how different it was from our dairy farm in Pennsylvania
3. the first thing we noticed was the color of the sky
4. the quality of light in the desert makes everything shine with clarity
5. have you seen the sun rise over an ancient Indian village
6. the air is so still and the undersides of the clouds so pink
7. listen you can almost hear the sounds of morning activity in the ancient Pueblo square
8. i wonder what life must have been like here long ago
9. have you noticed how difficult it is to breathe at this altitude
10. have you ever wondered about life in a swamp
11. what a paradise swamps are for plant life
12. think about the beautiful water hyacinth

13. do you know why this plant never gets waterlogged
14. the water hyacinth has a waxy skin
15. how amazing those mangrove trees are
16. can they actually grow in salt water
17. look carefully at the next-to-lowest branch on the right
18. do you see the iguana sunbathing
19. how incredible its camouflage is
20. is that a log floating in the water
21. no. that's a caiman, a creature related to the alligator
22. wow, I'm sure glad I didn't step on him
23. there have been many reports of UFOs
24. have you ever had such an experience
25. no, I haven't
26. i have read some of the reports, though
27. has anyone seen the inside of a flying saucer
28. look carefully at that photograph
29. what an unusual background it has
30. what a sweeping view of the sky this is

Commas Within Sentences

Use commas after introductory words, phrases, and clauses.
Examples:

> *Yes*, it is time to go. *In my opinion*, that book is the best one. *After I read all the books*, I donated them to the library.

Use commas between words, phrases, and clauses in a series.
Examples:

> He can *wash, dry,* and *fold* the clothes. Sally traveled *by automobile, in a canoe, and on horseback.*

Use commas to set off appositives, nonrestrictive clauses, nouns of direct address, and parenthetical expressions from the rest of a sentence.
Examples:

> Our steward, *James Moreno*, speaks three languages. (appositive)
> The book, *which was written by Tomás Rivera*, is on the book report list. (nonrestrictive clause)
> Tell me what you said, *Angelina*. (noun of direct address)
> Her last name, *by the way*, is the same as yours. (parenthetical expression)

Use a comma between the two independent clauses of a compound sentence.
Example:

> My grandparents live in Coleman, but they visit quite often.

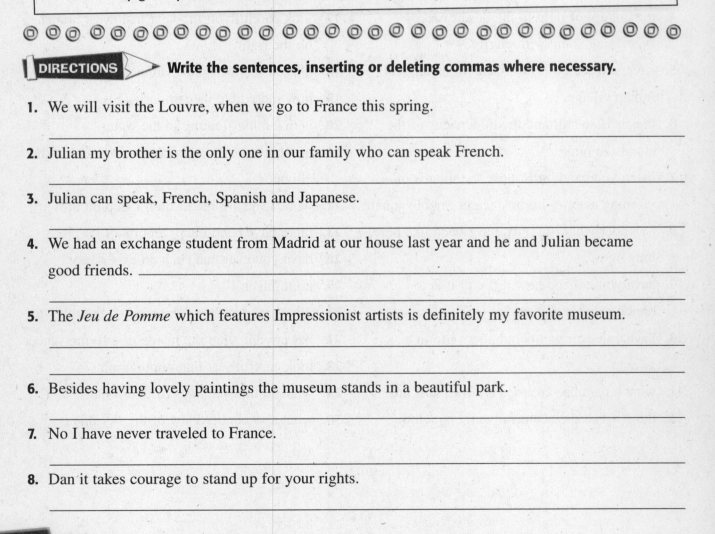

DIRECTIONS ▷ **Write the sentences, inserting or deleting commas where necessary.**

1. We will visit the Louvre, when we go to France this spring.

_____

2. Julian my brother is the only one in our family who can speak French.

_____

3. Julian can speak, French, Spanish and Japanese.

_____

4. We had an exchange student from Madrid at our house last year and he and Julian became good friends. _____

5. The *Jeu de Pomme* which features Impressionist artists is definitely my favorite museum.

_____

6. Besides having lovely paintings the museum stands in a beautiful park.

_____

7. No I have never traveled to France.

_____

8. Dan it takes courage to stand up for your rights.

_____

Other Punctuation Within Sentences

Use a **colon** between the hour and the minutes in time designations and after phrases that introduce a list.
Examples:
> It is 12:00. My report contains three paragraphs: the introduction, the body, and the conclusion.

Use **semicolons** in compound sentences and in sentences that have items in a series already separated by commas.
Examples:
> Frank scrubbed hard for two hours; at last the walls were free of dirt.
> The groups of actors in the first play were Anita, Margaret, and Patricia; and Moses, Danny, and Andrés.

Use a **dash** to show a sudden break in thought.
Example:
> Two officers—the president and the secretary—were absent.

Use a **hyphen** to divide a word at the end of a line and to write out the names of compound numbers and fractions.
Examples:
> twenty-two   three-fourths

Use **parentheses** to set off information not necessary for the meaning of the sentence.
Example:
> Blue (we call her that because she always wears that color) was eating in the restaurant.

DIRECTIONS Write each sentence, inserting needed punctuation.

1. The river rafters huddled under a tree it had been raining steadily for an hour.

_____

2. They had met at the Pancake House at 730 that morning.

_____

3. The two big rafts lay in a muddy puddle of water, and the provisions food, water, extra paddles, and sleeping bags were piled under a tarp.

_____

_____

4. One man looked glumly at the planned itinerary Roseville, Salamander Island, and Bishop's Gate.

_____

_____

5. If this trip were canceled and it looked as if it would be everyone would be disappointed.

_____

_____

6. The recipe called for one half cup of sugar and one fourth cup of flour.

_____

Numbers in Sentences

Spell out numbers that have fewer than three words or that begin sentences.
Examples:
> We used sixty-five bricks on our patio.
> Fifteen hundred people attended the concert.

Use numerals in dates, times, addresses, room numbers, and divisions of reading materials.
Examples:
> September 1, 1952   5:45 A.M.   9710 Chukar Circle   page 10

DIRECTIONS ▷ Write the correct numeral or number word from the parentheses.

1. Fire Island, a small spit of land off Long Island, is barely _____ (thirty, 30) miles long.

2. About _____ (12, twelve) or _____ (15, fifteen) communities line its beaches.

3. _____ (Two thousand; 2,000) weekenders visit the island during the summer season.

4. The winters are so harsh, barely _____ (sixty, 60) people inhabit the island.

5. In the _____ (nineteen thirties, 1930s) a catastrophic hurricane washed many of these seaside communities into the sea.

6. That tragedy was covered on page _____ (one, 1) of newspapers across the country.

7. Now, over _____ (two hundred, 200) homes are built on stilts to withstand the high tides that come every fall.

8. The house at _____ (sixteen, 16) Beach Plum Road even has a pool built on stilts.

9. Jan was staying in room _____ (eight hundred, 800).

10. _____ (Twenty, 20) teachers attended the meeting.

11. Abilene has a population of _____ (100,000; one hundred thousand) people.

12. The graduation ceremony begins at _____ (8, eight) o'clock.

DIRECTIONS ▷ Rewrite each sentence so that the number does not begin the sentence.

13. 250 miles to the north lies Cape Cod.

_____

14. 106 sailboats will race to the Cape this weekend.

_____

15. 532 crew members, coming from as far as the Caribbean, will take part in the race.

_____

_____

Capitalization of Proper Nouns, Proper Adjectives, and *I*

Capitalize a **proper noun**. A proper noun names a particular person, place, thing, or idea. If a proper noun is more than one word, do not capitalize unimportant words such as *of* or *the*.
Examples:

Ann Richards   Burnet Middle School   Gulf of Mexico

Capitalize a **proper adjective**. A proper adjective is formed from a proper noun. Many proper adjectives describe nationality or location.
Examples:

African traditions   Republican party   Scottish music

Capitalize **abbreviations** of proper nouns and proper adjectives, and end most abbreviations with a period.
Examples:

Dr. Laura Flawn   TX   Ms.

Capitalize the pronoun *I*.
Example:

Sammy and *I* are eating a salad.

 **DIRECTIONS** Circle each letter that should be capitalized. Write the capital letter above it. Draw a line through each capital letter that should be lowercase. Write the lowercase letter above it.

1. A Multinational team of Explorers is leaving for the north pole some tuesday in the spring.

2. My Friend captain wilkins will begin his voyage to the arctic circle with the other Explorers on a special Ship.

3. Before the Ship leaves, senator Reyna will read a proclamation from the united nations in english, russian, french, and chinese.

4. As the Ship passes under the golden gate bridge, i will wave Good-bye to my Friend Dan.

5. Once they leave the Ship, the Explorers will travel North using Dogsleds made in canada.

6. In our school, mr. ming's class will follow the expedition.

7. The greek parthenon in athens had a great effect on later Architectural styles.

8. Early roman Architects borrowed heavily from the greeks.

9. The romans also borrowed from the etruscans and the asians, who built Semicircular arches and vaults.

DIRECTIONS Write either the proper adjective (adj.) or the abbreviation (abbr.) for each word.

10. Greece (adj.)_____

11. Senator (abbr.) _____

12. South America (adj.) _____

13. Alaska (abbr.) _____

14. Italy (adj.) _____

15. Canada (adj.) _____

Abbreviations

An **abbreviation** is a shorter way to write a word. Do not capitalize abbreviations for common nouns.
Examples:

      in. (inches)   Ave. (Avenue)

Capitalize abbreviations that stand for proper nouns.
Examples:

      Oct. (October)   Sr. (Senior)

Do not use periods when writing postal abbreviations of the fifty states or the abbreviations of some large organizations.
Examples:

      NH (New Hampshire)   NBA (National Basketball Association)

Do not use periods with certain measurements.
Examples:

      cm (centimeter)   km (kilometer)

DIRECTIONS Write the meaning for each abbreviation.

1. USA or U. S. A. _____
2. UN _____
3. NATO _____
4. tbsp. or T. _____
5. tsp. or t. _____
6. Co. _____

7. Mr. _____
8. V.P. _____
9. Capt. _____
10. MO _____
11. lb _____
12. mph _____

DIRECTIONS Write the abbreviation for each word or phrase.

13. milliliter _____
14. Master of Science _____
15. Avenue _____
16. kilogram _____
17. Circle _____
18. ounce _____
19. New Jersey _____
20. Doctor _____
21. Incorporated _____
22. Junior _____
23. yard _____
24. milligram _____

25. liter _____
26. cubic centimeter _____
27. Boulevard _____
28. Road _____
29. National Collegiate Athletic Association

    _____

30. revolutions per minute _____
31. Fahrenheit _____
32. Celsius _____
33. New York _____
34. Sunday _____

Letters

A **friendly letter** has five parts. Use correct capitalization for letter writing.

The **heading** contains the address of the person writing the letter and the date.

The **greeting** tells to whom the letter is written. Use a comma after the greeting in a friendly letter.

The **body** is the message of the letter. Indent each paragraph.

The **closing** is the ending that follows the body.

The **signature** is the name of the person who is writing the letter.

DIRECTIONS ⟹ Rewrite the letter with the correct capitalization, punctuation, and indentation.

36 Oakly Road
Hornell, New York

14802
October 5, 2003

dear janet:
College is such a new experience! It's taken me a month to get used to all the new routines. It's also a little scary. Sometimes I miss being home.
Write soon and tell me all about Ridge High. I'll see you at Thanksgiving.

regards:
angie

_____

_____

_____

_____

_____

_____

_____

_____

_____

_____

_____

_____

Titles

Capitalize the first word, the last word, and all important words in a title.
Underline the titles of books, plays, magazines, newspapers, television shows, movies, and works of art and music. Italicize the titles if you are using word processing software.
Examples:
<u>The Secret Garden</u>   <u>Los Angeles Times</u>   <u>60 Minutes</u>   <u>Pinocchio</u>
Place quotation marks around the titles of short works such as poems, short stories, chapters, articles, and songs.
Examples:
"The Raven"   "To Make a Prairie"   "Building a Bird Feeder"   "America"

DIRECTIONS Rewrite each sentence. Capitalize and punctuate titles correctly.

1. I read an article in esquire magazine yesterday.

   _____

2. It was titled senior prom revisited.

   _____

3. The writer is a well-known reporter for the sacramento bee.

   _____

4. The article contained an excerpt from the book going home again.

   _____

5. Everyone was curious about a sculpture called locker that stood in the gymnasium.

   _____

6. One man brought a video crew from the television program you are there.

   _____

7. Where is last week's issue of time?

   _____

8. Have you read John Steinbeck's book travels with charley?

   _____

9. I just found that article, welcome to pittsburgh.

   _____

10. Have you seen the movie beauty and the beast?

    _____

11. My family enjoys watching Monday night football.

    _____

Direct Quotations and Dialogue

Use quotation marks before and after a **direct quotation**. Separate the quotation from the rest of the sentence with a comma or other punctuation. Place a comma or a period inside closing quotation marks.
Example:

"The truth is powerful and will prevail," said Sojourner Truth.

If a quotation is interrupted by other words, place quotation marks around the quoted words only.
Example:

"The truth is powerful," said Sojourner Truth, "and will prevail."

Place a question mark or an exclamation point inside closing quotation marks if the quotation itself is a question or an exclamation.
Example:

"Haven't you heard of Sojourner Truth?" asked Marcia.

To write **dialogue in a narrative**, write each person's exact words within quotation marks and begin a new paragraph each time the speaker changes.
Examples:

"Please give me the map," said Gabriela.

"I need it right now. I'll give it to you later," said Kay.

To write **dialogue for a play**, list all speakers' names before their words and put a colon after their names.
Examples:

Patrick: Give me liberty or give me death!

Ben: I have heard those words before.

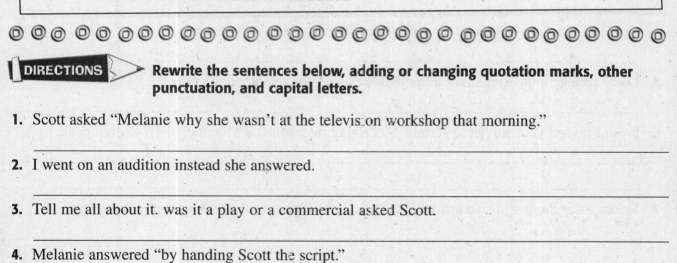

DIRECTIONS Rewrite the sentences below, adding or changing quotation marks, other punctuation, and capital letters.

1. Scott asked "Melanie why she wasn't at the television workshop that morning."

_____

2. I went on an audition instead she answered.

_____

3. Tell me all about it. was it a play or a commercial asked Scott.

_____

4. Melanie answered "by handing Scott the script."

_____

5. girl (Reading a book while riding a skateboard) who said bookworms are square?
announcer: january is National Library Month. escape with a book!

_____

_____

6. Wow Scott yelled "as he read the script. A commercial!

_____

Appositives

An **appositive** identifies or renames the noun or pronoun that precedes it. Use commas to set off an appositive from the rest of the sentence.
Examples:
>   His home is in Rome, the *capital of Italy*.
>   The pilot, *Captain Singrossi*, said to fasten our seat belts.

DIRECTIONS ▷ **Rewrite each sentence inserting commas where needed. Then underline the appositive and write the noun or nouns it explains or renames.**

1. Jerome once a thriving copper-mining town sits on the edge of Mingus Mountain in Arizona.
_____
_____

2. When the mine closed, Jerome became a ghost town a town without people.
_____

3. It remained that way for many years until artists, potters, and weavers people seeking a quiet lifestyle rediscovered Jerome.
_____
_____

4. Now the company "Made in Jerome" makes handsome pottery there.
_____

5. Local cottage industries small home-based businesses sell arts and crafts.
_____

6. From Prescott you can get to Jerome by driving over Mingus Mountain a 7,743-foot peak.
_____
_____

7. Madagascar the world's fourth-largest island lies off the coast of Africa in the Indian Ocean.
_____
_____

8. Portuguese explorers the first Europeans to see Madagascar landed there around 1500.
_____

9. Tom Brokaw an anchor on the evening news has retired.
_____

10. Two of my classes algebra and marketing were cancelled today.
_____

Homonyms and Homographs

Homonyms are words that sound alike but have different spellings and meanings.
Examples:
    their, they're, there   here, hear   a lowed, aloud
Homographs are words that are spelled alike but have different meanings and sometimes different pronunciations.
Examples:
    saw, meaning "a cutting tool"; *saw*, meaning "the past tense of *see*"

DIRECTIONS Choose the homonym in parentheses that fits in each sentence.

1. A crowd gathered around the black-caped man on the (beach, beech).

2. The onlookers screamed when he swallowed a (soared, sword).

3. The magician clutched his throat as if he were in great (pain, pane).

4. He began to (real, reel) as if he were going to (faint, feint).

5. Then he managed in some (manner, manor) to disappear into thin (air, heir).

6. What (flair, flare) this magician had!

7. He was a master of (sleight, slight) of hand.

8. Had the moon (shone, shown) brightly that night the patriots might have been discovered.

9. The (principle, principal) of our school is Mrs. Díaz.

10. The family's breakfast consisted of (wry, rye) bread, homemade jam, potted herring, and a hot drink made from chicory root.

DIRECTIONS Each word below is a homograph. Write two sentences showing two different meanings for each word.

11. tire

    a) _____

    b) _____

12. curb

    a) _____

    b) _____

13. refuse

    a) _____

    b) _____

14. close

    a) _____

    b) _____

Prefixes

A **base word** is a complete word that cannot be separated into smaller parts and still retain its meaning.
Examples:
> common   comfort   assure

A **prefix** is a word part added to the beginning of a base word to change its meaning.
Examples:
> un + common = *uncommon*
> dis + comfort = *discomfort*
> re + assure = *reassurance*

A prefix, like a base word, has a meaning of its own.
Examples:

prefix	meaning	prefix	meaning
un	not, opposite of	dis	opposite of, not
re	back, again	fore	before
in	not	mis	wrong
im	not	co	together
il	not	pre	before

DIRECTIONS > **Choose the word in parentheses to complete each sentence. Use a dictionary if you need help with prefix meanings.**

1. Five schools participated in the _____ games.
   (extracollegiate, intercollegiate)

2. Lakeview was _____ because one player _____
   (disqualified, misqualified)   (displaced, misplaced)
   her uniform.

3. _____, the team sat on the sidelines while the others competed.
   (Dejected, Interjected)

4. The team was _____, but the team members _____
   (disappointed, reappointed)   (interlooked, overlooked)
   her carelessness.

DIRECTIONS > **Add a prefix to each of the words below to make a new word. Write the new word on the line first. Then write a sentence using the new word.**

5. spell _____

_____

6. view _____

_____

7. shadow _____

_____

8. profit _____

_____

Suffixes

Suffixes are word parts added to the end of a base word to make a new word.
Suffixes often change the meaning of the base word.
Example:

   ful, meaning "full of," + the base word *color* = colorful, meaning "full of color."

Examples:

suffix	meaning	suffix	meaning
ish	of the nature of	ist	one skilled in
ous	full of	able	able to be
er	one who does	tion	art of
hood	state of being	ful	full of
ward	in the direction of	al	pertaining to
ness	quality of	ible	able to be
ment	act or process of	like	similar to

DIRECTIONS Read the sentences and find each word that contains a suffix. Circle the suffix and write the word's meaning on the line. Use a dictionary if you need help.

1. Many hours of exhaustive study have shown that sleep has several stages.

2. Sleep deprivation can make some subjects very irritable.

3. Others may have strong feelings of restlessness when asked to sleep.

4. We now know that sleep has a measurable effect on our brains.

DIRECTIONS Read the base words and the suffixes. Combine them to make four new words. Write the new words on the lines; then use each one in a sentence.

Base Words	agree	manage	treat	like	WORD BOX
Suffixes	able	ment	ty	ly	

5. _____

6. _____

7. _____

8. _____

Idioms

An **idiom** is a commonly used expression that means something other than the combined meanings of its individual words.

Example:

Xavier always stands up for his views means "Xavier always defends his views," not, "Xavier always stands up on his feet for his views."

DIRECTIONS Rewrite the sentences below, replacing the underlined idioms with the usual meaning of the words that make up the idiom.

1. Mrs. Stamper had a lot of irons in the fire.

_____

2. She had told so many people about the party that she felt like a broken record.

_____

3. She gave all the guests the green light to sneak into the basement.

_____

4. Mark was on cloud nine when everyone yelled, "Surprise!"

_____

5. Albert was in the doghouse, so he did not go to the party.

_____

DIRECTIONS Replace each incorrect idiom with the correct one.

6. the running round and round _____

7. raining cat and mouse _____

8. run rings inside _____

9. up in the dumps _____

10. off the ceiling _____

11. in the same ship _____

12. walking on vapor _____

13. in cold water _____

14. fly off the pan _____

15. put our heads apart _____

Subject-Verb Agreement

The subject and the verb of a sentence agree in number. Use singular verbs with singular subjects and plural verbs with plural subjects.
Examples:

The dog *runs* around the yard. The dogs *run* around the yard.

Compound subjects may take singular or plural verbs.
Examples:

Michelle and Lexi *call* Matthew every day.

Michelle or Lexi *calls* Matthew every day.

If one subject is singular and the other plural, the verb should agree with the subject closer to it.
Examples:

Neither the cat not the puppies *have* eaten yet.

Neither the puppies nor the cat *has* eaten yet.

DIRECTIONS Write the present-tense form of the verb in parentheses that agrees with each subject.

1. we (write) _____

2. I (find) _____

3. Sal or Amy (work) _____

4. Bill (say) _____

5. Mr. Ramos (talk) _____

6. the people (send) _____

7. music (seem) _____

8. the baby (cry) _____

9. the planets (is) _____

10. the bird (have) _____

11. dolphins (have) _____

12. my bike (do) _____

13. the women (hear) _____

14. NATO (have) _____

15. asteroids (orbit) _____

16. the athlete (box) _____

17. my friend (is) _____

18. my friends (is) _____

19. the light (flash) _____

20. the moon (hang) _____

21. Luke and Ben (read) _____

22. Mom or the children (hurry) _____

23. the artist (create) _____

24. the PTA (do) _____

25. the boy (drive) _____

26. the girls (drive) _____

27. Margaret or Lillie (eat) _____

28. the teacher (teach) _____

29. the painters (paint) _____

30. the police officers (walk) _____

Personal Narrative: Analyzing

In a **personal narrative,** the writer tells about a personal experience. A personal narrative is autobiographical, but it typically focuses on a specific event.

A personal narrative
• is written in the first-person point of view.
• reveals the writer's feelings and includes details.
• usually presents events in sequential order.

⊚ ⊚⊚ ⊚⊚ ⊚⊚⊚ ⊚⊚⊚ ⊚⊚⊚ ⊚⊚⊚ ⊚⊚⊚ ⊚⊚⊚ ⊚⊚⊚ ⊚⊚⊚ ⊚⊚⊚ ⊚⊚ ⊚

> **DIRECTIONS** Rewrite the personal narrative below, putting the events in sequential order.

1. "Hello, Hello!" I screamed into the phone. Getting no answer, I jerked the receiver from my ear and stared at it, as if it could tell me who was on the other end. The telephone's piercing ring wrenched me awake yet again. I was so angry that I almost shouted. I clambered out of bed for the third time that evening. Disgusted, I slammed down the receiver. Whoever was calling and leaving me with silence would get a deafening whistle blast the next time my sleep was disturbed.

_____

_____

_____

_____

_____

_____

> **DIRECTIONS** Read the narrative and answer the questions.

2. What is the writer feeling and what details show this?

_____

_____

_____

_____

3. Read the last sentence of the paragraph again. Try to imagine what might happen next in the story, and add two sentences to show this.

_____

_____

_____

_____

⊚ ⊚⊚ ⊚⊚ ⊚⊚⊚ ⊚⊚⊚ ⊚⊚⊚ ⊚⊚⊚ ⊚⊚⊚ ⊚⊚⊚ ⊚⊚⊚ ⊚⊚⊚ ⊚⊚⊚ ⊚⊚⊚ ⊚

Personal Narrative: Visualizing Events and Feelings

To write a **personal narrative**, good writers picture the things that happened in sequential order and write details to show the reader what happened.

DIRECTIONS ▷ **Read the paragraph. Then answer the questions below.**

The crack of the bat promised a line drive to the outfield. I hopped back a step and raised my glove in anticipation. Suddenly, there was an explosion of light, and then everything went dark. I felt myself swirling in a tunnel. I heard a low-pitched moaning, faint, as though muffled in earth. I was surprised to realize that the sound was coming from me, Kate O'Reilly. When I opened my eyes and saw the white walls and white sheets, I knew I was in a hospital room. The pillow felt like rocks beneath my head. "What happened to the ball?" I croaked.

1. How did the writer answer the following questions?

Questions	Answers
Who?	_____
	_____
What?	_____
	_____
Where?	_____
	_____
Why?	_____
	_____
How?	_____
	_____

2. Which senses were detailed? Give an example of each.

Senses	Sensory Details
Sight	_____
	_____
Hearing	_____
	_____
Touch	_____
	_____

Personal Narrative: Proofreading

PROOFREADING HINT
To be a good proofreader, look for one type of error at a time. For example, proofread once for capitalization errors, once for punctuation errors, and once for spelling errors.

PROOFREADING MARKS

≡ Capitalize.
⊙ Add a period.
∧ Add something.
⋏ Add a comma.
∨∨ Add quotation marks.
⤺ Cut something.

⌃ Replace something.
∿ Transpose.
○ Spell correctly.
¶ Indent paragraph.
/ Make a lowercase letter.

 **DIRECTIONS** ▷ **Proofread the personal narrative, paying special attention to paragraph indentations. Use the proofreading marks to correct at least fifteen errors.**

I stood nervously at the water's edge with the rest of the racers. I checked and rechecked my suit and goggles. I stared across the lake, hoping to sight some secret about the race. I can remember now that I was shivering, but I had no sensation of cold. We were all to scared to be cold. The crowd seemed nosiy, restless. Then suddenly everyone was still.

At the sound of the gun there was pandemonium. The water churned with elbows, knees, and foot. I felt as if i were drowning. I couldn't catch my breath. I actually began to think of hanging back. perhaps I should wait for the others to take the lead and then try to catch up. Suddenly, one of my old swimming rivels passed me.

Galvanized, I set my coarse for the finish line. The familiar sound of water whooshing passed my ears was reassuring. I found my rhythm and settled into it. Breathe, kick, stroke; breathe, kick, stroke. don't think about it; just keep going. Now all that mattered was passing was passing the swimmers in front of me.

I felt must have been swimming for hours. I became disoriented, for I could see no one around me. Had the other swimmers left me so far behind Had I strayed into the wrong part of the lake? Still I continued breathing, kicking, stroking, trying not to think. I could hear a distant roaring. I only kept swimming; I had become a robot. When my stomach scraped sand, I stood up shakily. The roaring became cheering, and I new I had won the race.

Personal Narrative: Graphic Organizer

 **DIRECTIONS** Think about someone you know who is special to you. Write a personal narrative about this person. Use examples and details to show why this person is special. Use this writing plan to develop the content of your narrative.

WRITING PLAN

> Who is the person you will write about?

> Tell what makes this person special to you.

> Give examples to show why this person is special.

Personal Narrative: Writing

Tips for Writing a Personal Narrative:
- Write from your point of view. Use the words *I* and *my* to show your readers that this is your story.
- Think about what you want to tell your reader.
- Organize your ideas into a beginning, middle, and end.
- Write an interesting introduction that "grabs" your readers.
- Write an ending for your story. Write it from your point of view.

DIRECTIONS ▷ Write a personal narrative about someone you know who is special to you. Use the graphic organizer on page 89 as a guide for writing. Be sure to proofread your writing.

_____

_____

_____

_____

_____

_____

_____

_____

_____

_____

_____

_____

_____

_____

_____

_____

_____

_____

_____

_____

_____

_____

_____

Continue on your own paper.

How-to Paragraph: Analyzing

A **how-to paragraph** names the process, identifies the materials used, and lists the steps in the process.

DIRECTIONS Read the how-to paragraph below. Then answer the questions.

Fight mildew on a painted surface as soon as you discover it. Since it is a growth, you must kill the molds that cause mildew, or it will grow back. To clean mildew off painted surfaces, first mix one cup of liquid laundry bleach with two quarts of water. Add two tablespoons of a powdered cleanser. Then, scrub on the mixture with a toothbrush or scrub brush and allow it to dry on the surface. Last, rinse off the mixture thoroughly with plenty of water. You can repaint the surface when it is completely dry.

1. What process is named in the paragraph?

_____

_____

2. List and number the steps the writer included to perform this process.

_____

_____

_____

3. Make a list of the materials needed for this process.

_____

_____

_____

4. What materials, if any, are needed for this how-to but are not mentioned in the paragraph?

_____

_____

5. What details did the writer include to help the flow of the paragraph but are not absolutely essential?

_____

_____

_____

How-to Paragraph: Evaluating to Select Essential Information

To write a **how-to paragraph**, skilled writers evaluate the possible steps and details and include only those necessary to explain the process.

DIRECTIONS > Read the topic sentence and the steps following it. Next to each step, write *E* if the information is essential or *U* if the information is unnecessary. Tell why you think the step is unnecessary.

Diving safely requires preparing yourself and your equipment.

_____ **1.** Diving is the way that people enter the underwater world.

_____

_____ **2.** Assemble your gear next to your air tank.

_____

_____ **3.** Fins that are too large will make you tire quickly.

_____

_____ **4.** Check the pressure gauge on your tank to be sure that your tank contains the necessary amount of air.

_____

_____ **5.** Next, check for leaks and tighten all valves.

_____

_____ **6.** A leaky valve will cause your air supply to run out more quickly than you expect.

_____

_____ **7.** Attach your tank to your stabilizing jacket before you suit up.

_____

_____ **8.** This eliminates having to attach your tank after your jacket is on.

_____

_____ **9.** To avoid cramped or pulled muscles in the water, perform mild stretching exercises before suiting up.

_____

_____ **10.** Hold your mask firmly with one hand and secure your regulator in your mouth with the other as you enter the water.

_____

_____ **11.** Diving suits are used by some divers because they reduce the loss of body heat and allow the diver to stay underwater for longer periods.

_____

How-to Paragraph: Proofreading

PROOFREADING HINT
To be a good proofreader, look for one type of error at a time. For example, proofread once for capitalization errors, once for punctuation errors, and once for spelling errors.

PROOFREADING MARKS

≡ Capitalize.	⌄ Replace something.
⊙ Add a period.	ᵕ Transpose.
∧ Add something.	◯ Spell correctly.
⋏ Add a comma.	¶ Indent paragraph.
⋁⋁ Add quotation marks.	╱ Make a lowercase letter.
✂ Cut something.	

 Proofread the how-to paragraphs, paying special attention to the capitalization and end punctuation of sentences. Use the proofreading marks to correct at least fourteen errors.

How often during the day do you feel tense Do the stresses of being a student, a friend, a son or a duaghter, an athlete or a musician sometimes seem too much for you? you probably need to take a few minutes and relax Using specific relaxation techniques can help you.

In order to learn relaxation techniques, you need only a quiet room and a comfortable place to sit or recline. Before you settle yourself, you may want to darken the room slightly.

begin by closing your eyes and breathing deeply. in through your nose and out threw your mouth. do this three or four times feel your breath entering your body. Then imagine your breath traveling through all your muscles, relaxing them. Imagine that you are lying on a warm beach or in a fragrant meadow. As you continue breathing. think of each part of you're body relaxing. Notice how heavy your legs are becoming. Feel each vertebra in your spine loosen and relax Feel the knots in your shoulders loosen, and imagine a soft Summer breeze blowing through your hair. You may even begin to feel as if you are floating. This means you are achieving relazation.

try this technique every time you feel tense. Relaxation exercises can help you perform your everyday tasks a bit more productively and can help you feel refreshed.

How-to Paragraph: Graphic Organizer

 Think about something you want to tell others how to do. Use this writing plan to help you develop the content of your paragraph.

WRITING PLAN

What will you tell others how to do?

List the materials that will be needed.

Write the steps of the task in order. Number them.

List some sequence words that will help the reader know what to do.

How-to Paragraph: Writing

> **Tips for Writing a How-to Paragraph:**
> • Choose one thing to teach someone.
> • Think of all the materials that will be needed.
> • Think of all the steps in the task.
> • Use sequence words in your directions.

DIRECTIONS ▷ Write a how-to paragraph about something you want to tell others how to do. Use the graphic organizer on page 94 as a guide for writing. Be sure to proofread your writing.

_____

_____

_____

_____

_____

_____

_____

_____

_____

_____

_____

_____

_____

_____

_____

_____

_____

_____

_____

_____

Continue on your own paper.

Compare and Contrast Paragraph: Analyzing

A **compare and contrast paragraph**
- describes the similarities or difference in two or more items or describes their advantages and disadvantages.
- addresses the same features or questions about each subject.
- is organized in a subject-by-subject or a feature-by-feature method.

DIRECTIONS **Read the following paragraphs. Underline the topic sentence in each paragraph. Answer the questions.**

The wastelands of Antarctica and the Sahara in Africa are entirely different kinds of deserts. Antarctica is a continent that is virtually covered by an ice cap up to thirteen thousand feet thick. Summer temperatures rarely rise above zero degrees Fahrenheit, and in winter, the temperature plummets to minus seventy degrees Fahrenheit. Antarctica is surrounded by miles of ice-encrusted ocean. In contrast, the Sahara covers a large area of North Africa and is made up of burning sand dunes and gravel. Daytime temperatures in the Sahara reach 135 degrees Fahrenheit in the shade. The Sahara is surrounded by land and sea.

1. Does this paragraph compare or contrast the two deserts? How do you know?

   _____

   _____

   _____

2. Is the subject-by-subject or feature-by-feature method used to organize the ideas?

   _____

   _____

Singers and athletes have much in common. Singers must practice breath control in order to sustain notes. In the same way, athletes, especially weight lifters, must regulate their breathing to lift heavy stacks of weights. Even though singers don't run races, they must have enormous stamina to project their voices without the aid of a microphone. Athletes must be in top condition, too, in order to compete successfully.

3. Does this paragraph compare or contrast singers and weight lifters? How do you know?

   _____

   _____

   _____

4. Is the subject-by-subject or feature-by-feature method used to organize the ideas?

   _____

   _____

Compare and Contrast Paragraph: Evaluating Whether to Compare or Contrast

To write a **compare and contrast paragraph**, skilled writers group details into categories. Then, writers evaluate the categories to decide which kind of paragraph to write and which details to include.

DIRECTIONS Write the most important thing the two items in each pair have in common.

1. desktop computers and laptop computers _____

2. North America and South America _____

3. trains and boats _____

4. mittens and hats _____

DIRECTIONS Fill in the Venn diagrams below for the topics given. Show at least two similarities and two differences for the items.

5. cassette tapes and music CDs

6. crayons and pencils

Compare and Contrast Paragraph: Proofreading

PROOFREADING HINT
To be a good proofreader, look for one type of error at a time. For example, proofread once for capitalization errors, once for punctuation errors, and once for spelling errors.

PROOFREADING MARKS

≡ Capitalize.

⊙ Add a period.

∧ Add something.

⩒ Add a comma.

⩔⩔ Add quotation marks.

⤲ Cut something.

⤳ Replace something.

⤯ Transpose.

◯ Spell correctly.

¶ Indent paragraph.

╱ Make a lowercase letter.

DIRECTIONS — Proofread the compare and contrast paragraph, paying special attention to sentence fragments and run-on sentences. Use the proofreading marks to correct at least ten errors.

Although the rococo style of art and architecture developed out of the baroque style, the two were quite different the baroque style developed in europe, England, and Latin America during the sixteenth and seventeenth centuries. Its essential design characteristics. Were based on a grand scale. Words such as *drama* and *energy* are often used to describe paintings and buildings in the baroque style examples of baroque architecture include Versailles in Paris and Christopher Wren's churches in England. Some of the European churches and monuments built in the baroque style are allmost overwhelming in their multitude of forms. Rococo is usually considered. A much more relaxed and intimate style than baroque. In contrast with the heavy grandness of baroque, the rococo style is more refined and delicate. Designs using shells, scrolls, branches and flowers appeared on furniture, tapestries, and sculptures throughout eighteenth century Europe rococo artists also used elements of Oriental art in their designs. Many of the palaces and churches still standing in southern Germany and austria present outstanding examples of the rococo style another fine example can be seen in the furniture of Thomas Chippendale from london

Compare and Contrast Paragraph: Graphic Organizer

Many people around the world have special relationships with animals. In the United States, many people own dogs. Some are working dogs, such as dogs trained to assist blind people, police officers, or firefighters. Others serve as social companions to people in homes and hospitals. Learn more about how these dogs and their relationships with people are alike and how they are different.

Use the Venn diagram below to plan the content of your paragraph. Write the main ideas you will include next to the headings **Main Idea**. For each idea, list what is true only about A in the A circle. List what is true only about B in the B circle. List what is true about both A and B where the two circles overlap.

 **DIRECTIONS** Choose two kinds of dogs you want to write about. Call them A and B.

WRITING PLAN

A = _____   B = _____

Main Idea: _____

Main Idea: _____

Main Idea: _____

A   Both   B

Compare and Contrast Paragraph: Writing

Tips for Writing Compare and Contrast Paragraphs:
- Find information about your subjects.
- Organize the information you find into main ideas.
- Use details to explain each main idea.
- Explain how the subjects are alike.
- Explain how the subjects are different.
- Use the final paragraph to summarize your main ideas in a new way.

DIRECTIONS Compare and contrast two kinds of dogs. Use the graphic organizer on page 99 as a guide for writing. Be sure to proofread your writing.

_____
_____
_____
_____
_____
_____
_____
_____
_____
_____
_____
_____
_____
_____
_____
_____
_____
_____
_____
_____
_____
_____

Continue on your own paper.

Compare and Contrast Paragraph: Writing

Cause and Effect Paragraph: Analyzing

> A **cause and effect paragraph** may begin with a cause and list its effects or begin with an effect and list its causes.

DIRECTIONS **Read the two paragraphs below. Underline the topic sentence in each. Then answer the questions.**

Dara yawned all through first and second periods and fell asleep at her desk in chemistry today. Saturday night, Dara baby-sat for the DeRosarios until midnight. When she got home, she wasn't tired, so she read a few chapters of a book by her favorite mystery writer. On Sunday, Dara washed and waxed her father's car, and she played soccer in the afternoon. After dinner, Dara did her French homework with Jay until 10 P.M.

1. Is the topic sentence a cause or an effect?

_____

2. List the events in the detail sentences and write whether they are causes or effects.

_____

_____

_____

_____

The sirocco is a hot, steady wind that blows from the Libyan deserts. It is a familiar but dreaded yearly occurrence. This oppressive wind brings dust and rain across the Mediterranean. Tempers grow short during this relentless onslaught, and some people become ill.

3. Is the topic sentence a cause or an effect?

_____

4. List the events in the detail sentences and write whether they are causes or effects.

_____

_____

_____

_____

DIRECTIONS **Choose one of the paragraphs above and add one sentence of your own that is a cause or an effect.**

5. _____

_____

Cause and Effect Paragraph: Connecting Cause and Effect

To write a **cause-and-effect paragraph**, skilled writers mentally connect one event to a series of other events and ask themselves why or what happened to connect the events.

DIRECTIONS Read each group of phrases below. Decide which are causes and which are effects. Fill in the diagram for each group. On the lines below each diagram, write a sentence that explains the links among the phrases.

1. clothes fit better
improving your posture
better lung capacity

	↓	↓

_____

_____

2. eat whole grains
get more sleep
have more energy

	↓	↓

_____

_____

DIRECTIONS Using the diagram on the left as a model, arrange the phrases listed below in the blank diagram on the right. The first cause and the final effect are provided for you. Write a sentence about your diagram on the lines provided.

3. eat less   clothes fit   lose weight   less appetite

cause	↓	exercise more
effect / cause	↓	
effect / cause	↓	
effect		more self-confidence

_____

_____

Cause and Effect Paragraph: Proofreading

PROOFREADING HINT
To be a good proofreader, look for one type of error at a time. For example, proofread once for capitalization errors, once for punctuation errors, and once for spelling errors.

PROOFREADING MARKS

≡ Capitalize.
⊙ Add a period.
∧ Add something.
⋏ Add a comma.
ⱽⱽ Add quotation marks.
⤙ Cut something.

⌃ Replace something.
ᔥ Transpose.
◯ Spell correctly.
¶ Indent paragraph.
／ Make a lowercase letter.

 **DIRECTIONS** — Proofread the cause and effect paragraphs, paying special attention to the correct use of verbs. Use the proofreading marks to correct at least ten errors.

The death of body tissues from a lack of oxygen are called gangrene. There is three distinct types of gangrene, each with a specific cause.

The most common form of this disorder is dry gangrene, which is caused by a gradual loss of blood supply. As the blood supply diminished, the body tissues fail to receive crucial nutrients. Unless the process of loss is reversed, the tissue slowly died. Dry gangrene may be the result of an illness such as diabetes or arteriosclerosis. It may also result from frostbite, which is caused by expozure to cold. The hands, feet, ears, and nose is the body parts most often affected.

Moist gangrene is a much more serious condition. It was caused by a sudden loss of blood supply to part of the body This sudden loss is typically the result of a wound or burn. Certain kinds of blood clots may also cause a sudden loss of blood and resulted in moist gangrene. The affected body part becomes infected, and the infectsion may spread spread to other parts of the body.

The third form of gangrene, now rather uncommon, was especially dangerous. Gas gangrene is caused by specific bacteria within a wound. Gas gangrene must be treated as soon as possible; untreated gas gangrene can cause death within a few days.

Cause and Effect Paragraph: Graphic Organizer

DIRECTIONS Think about an event in nature that involves a chain of causes and effects. Use this writing plan to help you write paragraphs of cause and effect.

CAUSE   EFFECT

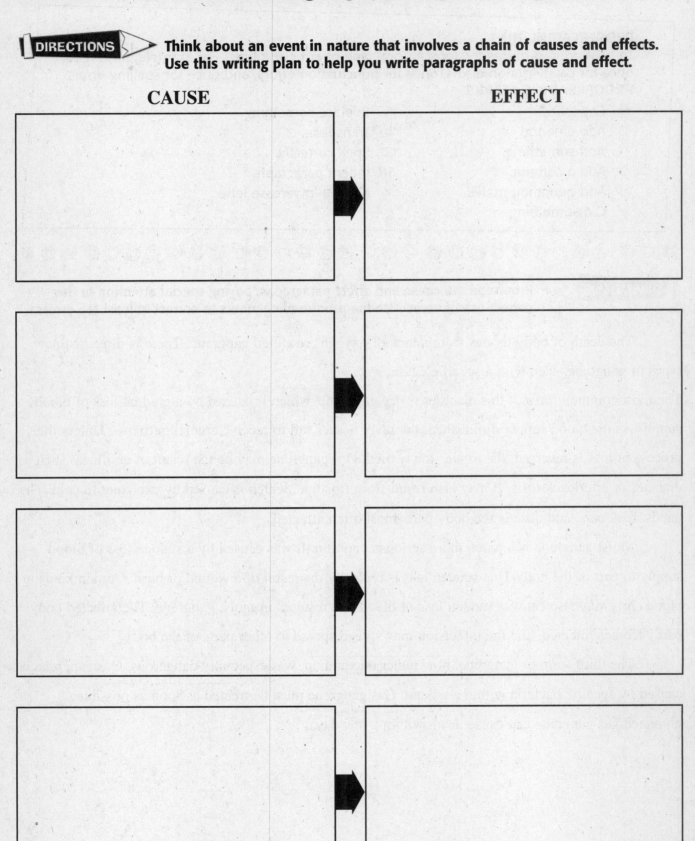

Cause and Effect Paragraph: Writing

Tips for Writing Cause and Effect Paragraphs:
- Begin paragraphs of effect with a cause. Write a topic sentence that tells what happened. The detail sentences should all discuss effects.
- Begin paragraphs of cause with an effect. Write a topic sentence that tells a result. The detail sentences should all discuss causes.
- Write detail sentences in the order in which the effects or the causes happened.

DIRECTIONS Write a cause and effect paragraph about an event in nature. Use the graphic organizer on page 104 as a guide for writing. Be sure to proofread your writing.

_____

_____

_____

_____

_____

_____

_____

_____

_____

_____

_____

_____

_____

_____

_____

_____

_____

_____

_____

_____

_____

_____

Continue on your own paper.

Persuasive Essay: Analyzing

A **persuasive essay** presents evidence to support one side of an issue and has an introduction, supporting arguments, and a conclusion.

 **DIRECTIONS** Underline the writer's thesis statement in each of the following introductions.

1. Traffic in downtown Tremont is straining services and tempers to the breaking point. Construction of Interstate 3 should begin immediately to divert trucks from already-clogged local streets. Ground-breaking, however, will not be without problems.

2. The bicycle helmet law now in effect is the sanest law the state has passed this year. Despite protests from some groups, most cyclists are complying with the month-old law. Serious injuries are down.

3. Thousands of dolphins are killed each year in tuna fishers' dragnets. Whales have also fallen prey to the nets. An alternative means of netting must be instituted to save protected species.

DIRECTIONS Read the following sections of a persuasive essay. Write *introduction*, *supporting argument*, or *conclusion* to identify them.

4. Cooperation is the cornerstone of success. Studies by citizen groups have proven that carpooling not only contributes to cleaner air, but also spells shorter commuting times.

_____

5. Many of our cities, even our smaller ones, are being choked by pollution. Most of this pollution is caused by cars. Carpooling can reduce the number of cars emitting these noxious fumes.

_____

6. Unfortunately, getting people to cooperate has been difficult. The image of the independent driver, responsible to no one, fades slowly. But people must be convinced that even one car pool can make a difference.

_____

7. Everyone wants to improve our quality of life, to preserve our environment, and to spend more time being productive. Carpooling is one answer to those goals.

_____

DIRECTIONS Answer the following questions about the sections of the essay above. Use complete sentences.

8. What is the thesis statement in the introduction?

_____

9. Which supporting argument paragraph would you put first and why?

_____

Persuasive Essay: Evaluating Reasons to Support a Conclusion

To write a **persuasive essay**, skilled writers develop conclusions based on reasons and provide evidence to support their conclusions.

DIRECTIONS ▷ Writers of persuasive essays must be able to determine whether statements are facts or opinions. Read the statements below. Next to each one, write *fact* or *opinion*.

1. More than two hundred cars cross Bay Creek Bridge per hour. _____

_____

2. The bridge charges a fifty-cent toll. _____

_____

3. This is a very cheap toll. _____

_____

4. Because the heavy traffic the bridge sustains has weakened it structurally, the bridge is in need of repair. _____

_____

5. The City Planning Commission has proposed raising the toll. _____

_____

6. The City Planning Commission is wrong. _____

_____

7. I would pay a toll to cross Bay Creek Bridge. _____

_____

DIRECTIONS ▷ Imagine you are trying to gather support for a weekend cleanup of a local river. Fill in the facts to support your reasons. The first one has been done for you.

8. Reason 1: The river is dirty.

Fact 1A: Bottles and cans are everywhere.

Fact 1B: _____

Reason 2: The river is an important water source.

Fact 2A: _____

Fact 2B: _____

Reason 3: The river supports a delicate balance of plants and animals.

Fact 3A: _____

Fact 3B: _____

Reason 4: The river is an important source of recreation for the community.

Fact 4A: _____

Fact 4B: _____

Persuasive Essay: Proofreading

 **DIRECTIONS** > **Proofread the persuasive essay, paying special attention to comparisons. Use the proofreading marks to correct at least fifteen errors.**

The Saturday recreation program at salisbury School should be reinstated. This program was clearly one of the successful in the School's history. Of all the recreation classes, the gymnastics classes were more popular. However, the other classes, especially those in art, dance, volleyball, and soccer, were also consistently popular. The number of students who wanted to enroll was often greatest than the number of spaces available. Children of all ages looked forward to participating in these recreation activities. In addition, they enjoyed the oppotunity of spending saturdays with their friends and of making new friends in the recreation classes. An additional advantage was that no one was excluded; supplies were always provided for those who could not afford to by their own class materials These program advantages make one wonder why the Saturday recreation hours were discontinued at all. It is clear that many people in the comunity support reinstatement of the recreation program. Some have launched a donation drive to provide the school with more-needed uniforms and equipment. Others have offered her own time to supervise the general activities in the recreation area and to free the staff for teaching duties. Parents, educators, and children all agree that closing the recreation program has deprived members of the West Ridge community of valuable activities. Working toward the good of the Community is most important than trying to save a little money.

Persuasive Essay: Graphic Organizer

 **DIRECTIONS** Write a persuasive essay about a topic that is important to you. State your opinion clearly. Also offer important reasons for this opinion. Use this writing plan to develop the content of your essay.

WRITING PLAN

What will the topic of your essay be?

_____

_____

_____

What is your opinion on this topic?

_____

_____

_____

Reason 1

_____

_____

_____

_____

Why? Support your reason.

_____

_____

_____

_____

Reason 2

_____

_____

_____

_____

Why? Support your reason.

_____

_____

_____

_____

Reason 3

_____

_____

_____

_____

Why? Support your reason.

_____

_____

_____

_____

Persuasive Essay: Writing

Tips for Writing a Persuasive Essay:
- Grab your reader's attention in the first paragraph.
- State your opinion clearly.
- Support your opinion with clear examples.
- Present your examples from least important to most important.
- Use the last paragraph to summarize your report.
- Use your last paragraph to convince the reader you are right.

DIRECTIONS ▷ Write a persuasive essay about a topic that is important to you. Use the graphic organizer on page 109 as a guide for writing. Be sure to proofread your writing.

_____
_____
_____
_____
_____
_____
_____
_____
_____
_____
_____
_____
_____
_____
_____
_____
_____
_____
_____
_____
_____
_____

Continue on your own paper.

Character Sketch: Analyzing

A **character sketch** includes sensory details and figurative language.
A **simile** compares two unlike things, using *like* or *as*.
A **metaphor** compares two unlike things without using *like* or *as*.
Personification gives human qualities to ideas, objects, or animals.

DIRECTIONS Read the character sketch below, underlining the sensory details in the paragraph. Then answer the questions on the lines provided.

1. At the festival dinner, we reminisced about Uncle Alberto. His mountainous bulk could always be found near a radio droning a ballgame. We called him The Sleeping Giant because he snored like a buzz saw through any amount of noise. Once, we gathered around him shrieking "The Star-Spangled Banner" like a gaggle of alarmed geese. He slept like a stone. When he was awake, however, his laugh boomed at us constantly, in a pungent smell of garlic.

2. What senses did the writer include in the paragraph? List them, with an example of each.

    _____

    _____

    _____

3. List the figurative language used in the paragraph. Label each one *simile, metaphor,* or *personification.*

    _____

    _____

    _____

4. Choose one figure of speech. Explain what it means. Tell whether you think it creates a vivid mental picture and why.

    _____

    _____

    _____

    _____

    _____

    _____

Character Sketch: Visualizing Comparisons

To write a **character sketch**, skilled writers often visualize the person, isolate a feature or a personality trait, and compare the person to something with the same trait.
Example:
His iron grip, when he greeted you, was as strong as a steel trap.
grip : iron   **as**   trap : steel

| DIRECTIONS > **Read the sentences below. Then write an analogy that describes the comparison in each.**

1. His voice reverberated like a booming bass drum.
   _____

2. His stumpy gait reminded me of Snow White's short-legged dwarfs.
   _____

3. The crown of his bald pate gleamed like a shiny billiard ball.
   _____

4. Even the dogs, when they heard him coming, skittered like frightened rabbits running for cover.
   _____

| DIRECTIONS > **Choose three animals and three people you know well. Fill out the diagram below to create an analogy.**

Person or Animal	:	Feature	as	Object	:	Feature

5. _____ : _____ as _____ : _____
6. _____ : _____ as _____ : _____
7. _____ : _____ as _____ : _____
8. _____ : _____ as _____ : _____
9. _____ : _____ as _____ : _____
10. _____ : _____ as _____ : _____

Character Sketch: Proofreading

DIRECTIONS Proofread the beginning of the character sketch, paying special attention to the correct use of pronouns. Use the proofreading marks to correct at least ten errors.

At first glance, Natalie seems as graceful as a stork picking through weeds for food. Hers thin arms and sinewy legs jut awkwardly when her walks. Like a bird, however, Natalie is at more at home in the air, and when she dances she rarely remains on the ground for long. As she dances, Natalie becomes a soaring gull; her earthbound friends are left to stare up at she enviously.

Beneath Natalies seemingly frajile airborne beauty is an iron will. Practicing doggedly for hours, she bends and stretches; her muscles are bundles of effort. The partner with who she has been dancing for years is a wrung-out rag halfway through a typical practice session.

Natalie rarely talks about dancing; she prefers to practice or perform. After repeatedly refusing to answer my questions about hers dancing, Natalie finally invited me to visit a private class that she and her partner had scheduled. I watched as them spent hours revising and polishing, working and reworking. Haggerd with effort and disappointed with their progress, her slumped against the wall until she got a second wind. Natalie insisted that they keep working until each movement was right.

Two weeks after that class, myself saw their first performance of the finished dance. All sense of effort, every hint of work, had disappeared. Natalie seemed to be a comet streaking across the stage.

Character Sketch: Graphic Organizer

Character Sketch

 **DIRECTIONS** Write a character sketch about a fictional person or a TV character with whom you are familiar. Use verbal analogies to describe the subject of your sketch.

WRITING PLAN

Write the name of the character in the middle of the word web. Then write describing words that tell how your character looks, acts, moves, dresses, and sounds on the lines.

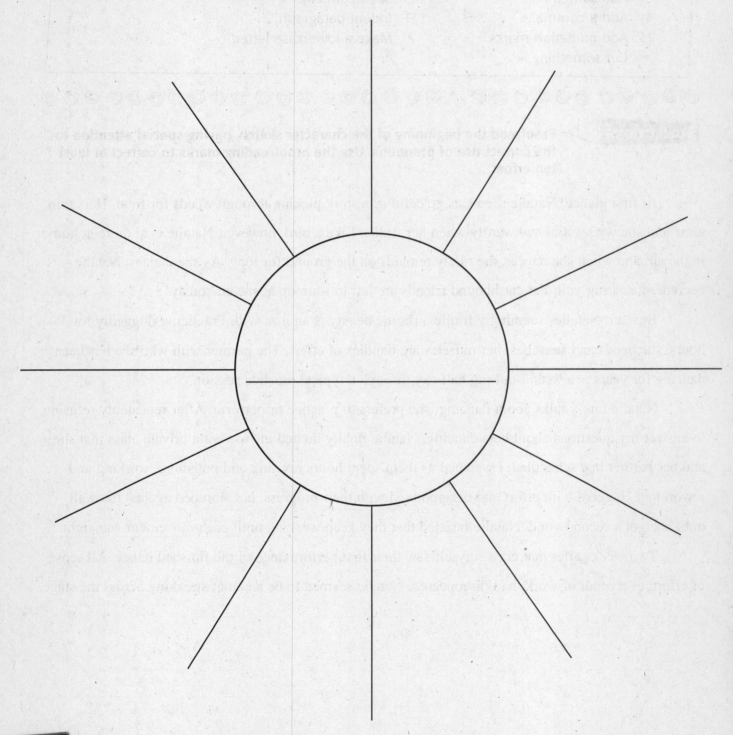

Character Sketch: Writing

Tips for Writing a Character Sketch:
- Write about someone you know or a character that you have created.
- Use verbal analogies to describe the subject of your sketch.
- Use images that appeal to two or more senses.

DIRECTIONS Write a character sketch about a fictional person or a TV character with whom you are familiar. Use the graphic organizer on page 114 as a guide for writing. Be sure to proofread your writing.

_____

_____

_____

_____

_____

_____

_____

_____

_____

_____

_____

_____

_____

_____

_____

_____

_____

_____

_____

_____

_____

_____

Continue on your own paper.

Short Report: Analyzing

A **short report** presents facts in an organized form, has a formal and serious tone, is based on source material, and has a title, introduction, body, and conclusion.

DIRECTIONS ▷ Write *yes* next to the topics below that are appropriate for a short report and *no* next to topics that are unsuitable. Write why they are unsuitable.

1. One Child's Prairie Christmas _____

_____

2. Major Holidays in the Balkans _____

_____

3. The History of the Arts and Crafts Movement _____

_____

4. Restaurant-Hopping with Hidayo _____

_____

5. How Movies Are Made _____

_____

DIRECTIONS ▷ Write two sentences adding to the body of the following report and one sentence to the conclusion. Read about the Nobel prize in an encyclopedia for more information.

6.   Alfred Nobel, a Swedish chemist and inventor, was involved in the development and manufacture of explosives. His invention of dynamite greatly improved the safety of using explosives. Oddly enough, Nobel was a pacifist. Concerned about the potential uses of the explosives he had invented, he established a fund. The fund was the basis of the Nobel prizes. They were established to reward those in the sciences, literature, and government whose work promoted international peace.

Body: _____

_____

_____

_____

_____

Conclusion: _____

_____

_____

Short Report: Connecting Ideas in a Summary

To write a **short report**, skilled writers summarize the information in their notes. Often, they summarize the main ideas of their report in the conclusion.

⊙ ⊙⊙ ⊙⊙ ⊙⊙⊙ ⊙ ⊙⊙ ⊙ ⊙⊙ ⊙ ⊙⊙⊙ ⊙ ⊙⊙ ⊙ ⊙⊙ ⊙ ⊙⊙⊙ ⊙ ⊙⊙ ⊙ ⊙⊙ ⊙ ⊙⊙ ⊙ ⊙⊙ ⊙

DIRECTIONS ▷ **Write a summary of the paragraph below.**

1.   *The Enlightenment* is a term for that period of time in the 18th century when scientific and intellectual thought blossomed. It was also known as the Age of Reason. Thinking during the Enlightenment was rational, liberal, humanitarian, and scientific. Outstanding thinkers of the 17th century, such as Francis Bacon and John Locke, emphasized natural law and universal order. Their beliefs gave rise to a sense of human progress and rationality. Benjamin Franklin and Thomas Jefferson are examples of influential Enlightenment thinkers.

_____

_____

_____

_____

_____

_____

_____

_____

_____

_____

_____

DIRECTIONS ▷ **Answer these questions about your summary.**

2. What is your main idea? _____

_____

3. What details support your main idea?_____

_____

_____

_____

_____

Short Report: Proofreading

 **DIRECTIONS** ▷ **Proofread the paragraphs from a short report, paying special attention to the correct use of prepositions. Use the proofreading marks to correct at least nine errors.**

Asteroids, also called minor planets or planetoids, were first discovered in the early nineteenth century. They are small irregularly shaped bodies that orbit the sun, most often among the orbits of Mars and Jupiter. Thousands of asteroids have already been observed, and astronomers continue to discover more.

The oval-shaped orbits of some asteroids occasionally bring these bodies quite near our planet, Earth Certain meteorite craters to Earth's crust may be the result from bombardment of the Apollo asteroids. Mining sites planned for these areas may bring us more information about the craters and the celestial bodies that caused them.

Scientists have considered various theories about the origin of asteroids, and it is likely that not all asteroids were formed in the same way. Asteroids may be fragments of a planet destroyed from the far past, or they may be material that failed to condense in a single planet. Some scientists believe that astaroids may be matter from the nuclei to ancient comets.

Asteroids vary greatly into size. The largest known asteroid is Ceres, which was discovered in 1801; its diameter is about 600 miles. Other large asteroids include Juno, Pallas, and Vesta. Icarus, discovered into 1949, is one of the smallest known asteroids; it has a diameter of just 0.6 miles.

Short Report: Graphic Organizer

 **DIRECTIONS** Write a short report about a science topic that interests you. Use this writing plan to develop the content of your report.

WRITING PLAN

The topic of this paper is:

_____

Main Idea of Paragraph 1: _____

_____

Detail: _____

Detail: _____

Detail: _____

Main Idea of Paragraph 2: _____

_____

Detail: _____

Detail: _____

Detail: _____

Main Idea of Paragraph 3: _____

_____

Detail: _____

Detail: _____

Detail: _____

Main Idea of Paragraph 4: _____

_____

Detail: _____

Detail: _____

Detail: _____

Short Report: Writing

Tips for Writing a Short Report:
- Find information about your topic.
- Take notes about main ideas important to your topic.
- Take notes about important details for each main idea.
- Organize the main ideas and details into paragraphs.
- Put paragraphs in a logical order.
- Use the last paragraph to summarize your report.

DIRECTIONS Write a short report about a science topic that interests you. Use the graphic organizer on page 119 as a guide for writing. Be sure to proofread your writing.

_____

_____

_____

_____

_____

_____

_____

_____

_____

_____

_____

_____

_____

_____

_____

_____

_____

_____

_____

_____

_____

Continue on your own paper.

Narrative Poem: Analyzing

A **narrative poem**, may be about a heroic event or a mock-heroic event, has narrative and poetic elements, and contains figures of speech and rhyme and rhythm.

DIRECTIONS Read the following selection. Then answer the questions or follow the directions.

The Wreck of the Hesperus

The skipper he stood beside the helm,
His pipe was in his mouth,
And he watched how the veering flaw did blow
The smoke now West, now South.

Then up and spake an old Sailor,
Had sailed to the Spanish Main,
"I pray thee, put into yonder port,
For I fear a hurricane."

—Henry Wadsworth Longfellow

1. Is "The Wreck of the Hesperus" a heroic or mock-heroic poem? Why?

_____

_____

2. How many stanzas are printed above and how do you know this?

_____

_____

3. Identify the kind of stanza in the poem. How do you know this?

_____

_____

4. Explain what you can of the story line.

_____

_____

5. Reread the excerpt above. Use marks to indicate the meter.

6. Now write the rhyme scheme at the ends of the lines.

Narrative Poem: Avoiding Wordy Language

Good writers make their writing concise by taking out unnecessary words or phrases and by substituting single words for long-winded phrases.

◎◎◎◎◎◎◎◎◎◎◎◎◎◎◎◎◎◎◎◎◎◎◎◎◎◎◎◎◎◎◎◎◎

DIRECTIONS ▷ **Edit the beginning of the poem below to remove the underlined words or replace them with shorter words or phrases.**

Clenched fist <u>tightly closed</u>

fingers curled <u>with stalwart</u>

<u>determination</u> around pen

eyes intent on <u>printed paper</u>

boring <u>great open holes</u>

through question sheet

forcing deep impressions on

<u>wooden school desk underneath</u>

Mind blank <u>not a thing inside</u>

<u>gazing eyes with a glaze over them</u>

far off

<u>legs and arms dancing freely</u> upon

hot sand kernels

lapping water upon <u>toes</u>

<u>immersed in cool ocean water</u>

escape <u>to summer vacation</u>

What <u>in the world</u> is the girl

in the red dress doing

looking <u>over and over</u> at the same line

for <u>about an hour</u>?

◎◎◎◎◎◎◎◎◎◎◎◎◎◎◎◎◎◎◎◎◎◎◎◎◎◎◎◎◎◎

Narrative Poem: Graphic Organizer

 **DIRECTIONS** ▷ **Think about a time you were courageous. Use this writing plan to develop the content of your poem.**

WRITING PLAN

Characters	Setting	Plot
Who are the characters?	What is the setting?	How will you describe the plot?
		Will you use dialogue?
		If so, what dialogue will you use?

Narrative Poem: Writing

Tips for Writing a Narrative Poem:
- Introduce the main character and the setting.
- Use description and dialogue to advance the plot.
- Use rhyme and rhythm for emphasis.
- Provide a satisfactory ending.

DIRECTIONS ▷ Write a narrative poem about a time you were courageous. Use the graphic organizer on page 123 as a guide for writing. Be sure to proofread your writing.

_____
_____
_____
_____
_____
_____
_____
_____
_____
_____
_____
_____
_____
_____
_____
_____
_____
_____
_____
_____
_____
_____

Continue on your own paper.

Using Parts of a Book

A **title page** tells the name of a book and its author.
A **copyright page** tells who published the book, where it was published, and when it was published.
The **preface** is an introductory statement or essay usually written by the author, explaining the scope, intention, or background of the book.
A **table of contents** lists the chapter or unit titles and the page numbers on which they begin. It appears at the front of a book.
A **glossary** is a list of words, with meanings, used in the book.
An **index** gives a detailed list of the topics in a book and the page numbers on which each topic is found. It is usually in the back of a book.

DIRECTIONS Imagine you are looking at a book about World War II. Decide which of the book parts you would use to find each piece of information. You may list more than one part for some answers.

1. descriptions of German war planes and the correct spellings of their names

_____

2. whether the information in the book is arranged chronologically, by battle, or by theater (area) of operation

_____

3. how up-to-date the book is compared to other books you have read on the same subject

_____

4. whether there are maps to show the Pacific Island battles

_____

5. information on Generals Eisenhower, MacArthur, and Rommel

_____

6. why the author wrote the book

_____

7. who published the book

_____

8. how many chapters are in the book

_____

9. the name of the author

_____

10. how many pages are in the glossary

_____

Using Parts of a Book, page 2

 **DIRECTIONS** Use the partial table of contents and index to answer the questions. If you answer a question with a page number or numbers, also identify the book part you used.

THE AMERICAN REVOLUTION

1. Where would you look to read the actual words of the Declaration of Independence?

_____

2. Where would you be likely to find information on King George III?

_____

3. Where would you look to see which came first, the Boston Massacre or the Boston Tea Party?

_____

4. Where would you be likely to find the names of George Washington's generals as well as the British military leaders?

_____

5. Where could you find a list of the duties and responsibilities of Congress and the executive branch?

_____

6. Where would you be likely to find reasons for the need for a new Constitution?

_____

Outlines and Bibliographies

Use an **outline** to organize main ideas and important details.
Use a Roman numeral for each main idea and a capital letter for each detail that supports the main idea.
Capitalize the first letter of every topic and detail.
Use a **bibliography** to list the sources used to gather information. The bibliography gives credit to the author of the material.
Examples:

> Willett, Edward. <u>Arthritis</u>. Berkeley Heights, NJ: Enslow Publishers, 2000. (book)
> "The Age of Arthritis." <u>Time</u>, Dec. 9, 2002, pp. 70–79. (magazine)

DIRECTIONS Unscramble and correctly rewrite the outline below. Put the title at the top of the first column.

African Grasslands
I.   plants of the grasslands
II.   animals of the grasslands
B.   grasses
A.   large predators
1.   lions and other cats
1.   giraffes
1.   ostriches
3.   eagles

A.   trees
C.   herbs
2.   hunting dogs
B.   large grazing animals
2.   zebras
2.   weaver birds
3.   elephants
C.   birds

_____   _____
_____   _____
_____   _____
_____   _____
_____   _____
_____   _____
_____   _____

DIRECTIONS Rewrite each bibliography entry correctly.

1. Bether Dvergsten Stevens—<u>Colorful Kites</u>. Logan, Iowa (2002), published by Perfection Learning

_____

2. "Unmasking Skin" by Joel L. Swerdlow. Pages 36–63 of the November 2002 <u>National Geographic</u>

_____

Using a Thesaurus

A **thesaurus** is a reference book that writers use to find the exact words they need. The thesaurus lists entry words alphabetically. Each entry word has a list of **synonyms**, or words that can be used in its place. Some thesauruses also list **antonyms** for the entry word.

Example:

You have just written the following sentence:
Spot **moved** the golf ball from the lake.
With the help of a thesaurus, you could improve the sentence by replacing **moved** with its more precise synonym **retrieved**.
Spot **retrieved** the ball from the lake.

DIRECTIONS ▷ **Use a thesaurus to rewrite each sentence, replacing words that are repeated or inexact.**

1. As the specter of revolution appeared ahead, rifts appeared even within families.

   _____

2. All of us spoke constantly of the uncertain future, and loyalists spoke in the marketplace about allegiance to Britain.

   _____

3. Those who were strongly in favor of rebellion preached just as strongly for their side.

   _____

4. Each side was convinced that its justifications were just.

   _____

5. The debating went on, until one day, as several of us stood debating on the green, we heard gunfire.

   _____

6. We all had the awful realization that an awful war was upon us.

   _____

DIRECTIONS ▷ **Use a thesaurus to rewrite each sentence, replacing each boldface word with a synonym.**

7. We are really enjoying our **trip** on this **elegant** ship.

   _____

8. We left Greenland, that **glimmering** land of snow, not too long ago.

   _____

9. We have seen **many** icebergs, and I'm hoping a **crash** does not **take place**.

   _____

Using a Dictionary

A **dictionary** lists words in alphabetical order, giving their pronunciation, part of speech, and definition. There are two **guide words** at the top of every dictionary page. The word on the left is the first word on the page, and the word on the right is the last word. Each word in the dictionary is an **entry** word, and it is divided into syllables.

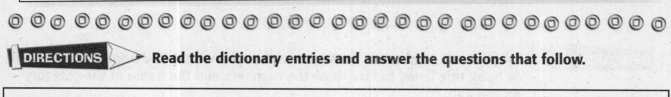

DIRECTIONS Read the dictionary entries and answer the questions that follow.

formation	forum

fort [fôrt] *n.* A structure or enclosed area strong enough to be defended against attack.

forte [fôrt] *n.* Something one does with excellence; strong point: Singing was her *forte*.

for·ti·fi·ca·tion [fôr′tə·fi·kā′shən] *n.* Something, like a wall or ditch, used for defense.

for·ti·fy [fôr′tə·fī] *v.* **for·ti·fied, for·ti·fy·ing 1** To make strong enough to resist attack. **2** To give added strength to; strengthen: Our hearty meal *fortified* us for the long trip ahead. **3** To add minerals or vitamins to.

for·ti·tude [fôr′tə·tōōd′] *n.* Courage to meet or endure danger.

for·tress [fôr′trəs] *n.* A fort or stronghold.

for·tu·nate [fôr′chə·nit] *adj.* Having or bringing good luck; lucky: a *fortunate* person or event. **—for·tu·nate·ly** *adv.* **—for·tu·nate·ness** *n.*

for·tune [fôr′chən] *n.* **1** Destiny; fate. **2** A person's future fate. **3** Luck or chance, whether good or bad: *Fortune* favored the successful actor. **4** Success. **5** A great sum of money; wealth.

1. What part of speech is *forte*? _____

2. What part of speech is *fortunately*? _____

3. Which syllable has the secondary stress in *fortification*? _____

4. What is the base word of *fortunately*? _____

5. Which meaning of the word *fortified* is used in the following sentence?
   Milk is often *fortified* with vitamin D. _____

6. What is the entry word for *fortunately*? _____

7. How many syllables does *fortification* have? _____

8. Would *formula* be found on a page with the guide words shown above? _____

9. Is this likely to be a page from the glossary of a book about defenses throughout history?
   Explain your answer. _____
   _____

Using the Library

Books are arranged on library shelves according to **call numbers**. Most school and public libraries use the Dewey decimal classification system to organize nonfiction books. Each nonfiction book is assigned a number from 000 to 999, according to its subject matter.

 **DIRECTIONS** Use the call numbers to determine where you would find books on each topic or book title listed below. Write the numbers and the name of the category on the line.

000–099 General Reference Books
(encyclopedias, atlases, newspapers)

100–199 Philosophy
(ideas about the meaning of life, psychology)

200–299 Religion
(world religion, mythology)

300–399 Social Sciences
(government, law, business, education)

400–499 Linguistics, Language
(dictionaries, grammar books)

500–599 Pure Sciences
(mathematics, chemistry, plants, animals)

600–699 Applied Sciences
(how-to books, engineering, radio)

700–799 Arts, Recreation
(music, art, sports, hobbies)

800–899 Literature
(poems, plays, essays)

900–999 History, Geography
(travel, biography)

1. Books about crocodiles and alligators _____

2. Books about filmmaking _____

3. Collections of plays _____

4. Books about Australia _____

5. Books about word origins _____

6. Books about religions of the world _____

7. Books about computer technology _____

8. *The First Heart Transplant* _____

9. *Psychology Through the Ages* _____

10. *Schooling in Japan* _____

11. *Amazon—the Mighty River* _____

12. *U. S. Interstate Road Atlas* _____

13. *Greece During the Golden Age* _____

14. *Neptune—The Blue Planet* _____

15. *Spanish: The Romance Language* _____

Using the Card Catalog

Libraries used to keep track of their inventory by having cards for each book. These cards were alphabetized and kept in **"card catalogs."** Most libraries now use **computerized card catalogs**. You can look up books by title, author, or subject. The computer can tell you whether the book is available or has been checked out.

DIRECTIONS ▷ **Explain how you would find the following information, using the system available in your library.**

1. You enjoyed reading a book on the Civil War by the author Bill Smith. How can you find out whether he has written books on the Revolutionary War period?

   _____

   _____

   _____

2. You want to see how many books your library has on James Forten. What do you do?

   _____

   _____

   _____

3. You want specific information on the Boston Massacre and the Boston Tea Party. Would you enter *American Revolution—subject* in the computerized card catalog? Why or why not?

   _____

   _____

   _____

4. You are looking for a specific book—*Pre-Revolutionary America* by Barbara Brown. You enter *Brown, Barbara—author* into the computerized card catalog. You learn there are three Barbara Browns who write books. Since you do not know which one she is, what do you do next?

   _____

   _____

5. Would you choose information by author, title, or subject to locate books about sports in Mexico?

   _____

6. Would you choose information by author, title, or subject to locate books written by Sandra Cisneros?

   _____

7. Would you choose information by author, title, or subject to locate the book *History of the Yurok*?

   _____

Using Reference Sources

> atlas—a book of maps
> thesaurus—a book of synonyms and antonyms
> dictionary—a book that gives the pronunciation and definitions of words
> almanac—a book that is published each year and gives facts about various topics such as the tides, weather, time the sun rises, etc. Much of the information is presented in charts, tables, and graphs.
> encyclopedia—a set of volumes that has articles about various topics
> *Books in Print*—a book that lists books that have been published about various subjects. Books are listed by author, by title, and by subject.

 Write the name of the reference source you would use to find each item of information. Some items may be found in more than one source.

1. the etymologies of the words *monarchy, aristocracy,* and *anarchy*

_____

2. a map of pre-Revolutionary War America

_____

3. titles of books by Milton Meltzer

_____

4. the current number of legislative representatives of each state

_____

5. synonyms and antonyms for the words *freedom* and *resistance*

_____

6. articles about American history

_____

7. historical data about the kings and queens of England

_____

8. biographies of Thomas Paine and Abigail Adams

_____

9. distances between major cities in the United States

_____

10. list of United States presidents and vice-presidents to the present time

_____

11. how many people live in Austin, Texas

_____

12. words to help you describe your excitement at seeing an alien

_____

13. the plight of elephants in Kenya and jaguars in the South American rain forests

_____

14. up-to-date statistics on disability benefits

_____

15. information on the Special Olympics

_____

Using the Internet

The **Internet** is an electronic connection to information and general data resources. The **World Wide Web** is a part of the Internet made up of millions of websites or webpages. A website or a webpage contains pictures, sounds, and video files. A **search engine** allows you to research the World Wide Web by using a keyword. When you enter a keyword, the search engine finds websites that contain that word. A **hyperlink** is a text or graphic that sends you to a new page or related website when you click on the link. The words in a hyperlink are underlined or are a different color from the rest of the text.
A **website address** can be used to go directly to a website. You can either type the website address or you can store it by bookmarking it as a favorite site.

DIRECTIONS ➤ **Use these three search engines to answer the questions.**

www.yahooligans.com   www.ajkids.com   www.altavista.com   **WORD BOX**

1. What is the African elephant's scientific name? Write the website address where you found the answer. When was this website last updated?

2. How much can the African elephant weigh? Write the website address and date of update.

3. Why is this animal an endangered species? Write the website address and date of update.

4. What are the African elephant's enemies? Write the website address and date of update.

5. How long is the African elephant's lifespan in the wild? In captivity? Write the website address where you found the answer. When was this website last updated?

6. How many site matches were listed for each search engine?

7. Which search engine gave you the best results? Which gave you the most results?

8. Which search engine was the hardest to use?

Core Skills: Language Arts, Grade 8

Answer Key

page 5
Answers will vary.

page 6
1. After the concert, all the altos went out for tacos., 2. There were three patios, but the singers couldn't decide where to sit., 3. Some sat beneath the overhanging branches of trees; others sat near the bushes., 4. The waiter brought them forks, spoons, and knives., 5. Then he asked if the women wanted tomatoes and avocados with their tacos., 6. Crab salads were served in halves of cantaloupes., 7. "We should all come back with our families," said one woman., 8. Most Saturdays, Margaret watches the orchestras play symphonies., 9. The costumes of the actors are very colorful and attractive., 10. The musicians play guitars, accordions, and violins.

page 7
1. trout, 2. deer, 3. oxen, 4. sheep, 5. shellfish, 6. waltzes, 7. fathers-in-law, 8. species, 9. capfuls, 10. heroes, 11. alumnus, 12. calves, 13. passerby, 14. teeth, 15. aspirin, 16. mouse, 17. woman, 18. attorneys-at-law, 19. die, 20. man, 21. When the foxes entered the barnyard, all the geese, chickens, and sheep panicked., 22. Before the children put an end to the turmoil, several crates of zucchini had been trampled., 23. My friends gave me three scarves for my birthday., 24. The editors-in-chief wrote the article about the computer glitches., 25. The men carrying the umbrellas had boxes of blueberries.

page 8
1. a teenager's music, 2. teenagers' music, 3. my neighbor's dog, 4. my neighbors' yard, 5. the car's dashboard, 6. the pencils' erasers, 7. Molly's pool, 8. Texas's history, 9. the brothers' bikes, 10. Agnes's fish, 11. my stepsister's street, 12. Amanda Jones's two cats, 13. the students' eyes, 14. Bess's contribution, 15. a witness's testimony, 16. children's ideas, 17. the eighth-graders' classroom, 18. construction workers' hats, 19. the Bodettes' cabin, 20. Rex's doghouse, 21. the elephants' tusks, 22. the story's ending

page 9
1. I—singular; we—plural, 2. it—singular, neuter, our—plural, 3. He—singular, masculine, 4. you—singular; it—singular, neuter; us—plural; I—singular, 5. I—singular, you—singular; he—singular, masculine; me—singular, 6. They—plural, 7. You—plural, 8. My—singular; them—plural, 9. Her—singular, feminine; us—plural, 10. theirs—plural

page 10
1. hostels and them; plural, neuter, 2. American Youth Hostels, Inc. and it; singular, neuter, 3. Members and they; plural, masculine or feminine, 4. hostels and they; plural, neuter, 5. Miranda and she; singular, feminine, 6. photographs and them; plural, neuter, 7. Miguel and he; singular, masculine, 8. Octavio, Carlos, and they; plural, masculine, 9. hostel and it; singular, neuter, 10. grandfather and he; singular, masculine

page 11
1. they, them, 2. I, 3. me, I, him, 4. I, 5. they, 6. she, 7. us, 8. He, 9. me, 10. her, 11. They, 12. She, 13. We, 14. them, 15. us

page 12
1. My, his, 2. her, 3. mine, my, 4. your, mine, 5. yours, mine, 6. his, 7. their, 8. his, 9. their, 10. her, 11. his, 12. his, 13. their, 14. its, 15. our, 16. My, 17. my, 18. mine, 19. your, 20. their

page 13
1. himself—reflexive, 2. These—demonstrative, 3. myself—reflexive, 4. itself—intensive, 5. yourself—reflexive, 6. yourselves—reflexive, 7. that—demonstrative, 8. myself—reflexive, 9. this—demonstrative, 10. that—demonstrative, myself— reflexive

page 14
1. was, 2. were, 3. their, 4. were, 5. was, 6. their, 7. themselves, were, 8. their, 9. were, 10. was, 11. was, 12. Does

page 15
1. who—relative pronoun, president, 2. that—relative pronoun, platitudes, 3. Who—interrogative pronoun; that—relative pronoun, message, 4. whom—interrogative pronoun, 5. whose—relative pronoun, candidate; who—relative pronoun, candidate, 6. correct, 7. Was it the person who spoke to us earlier?, 8. Whom can I trust with the ballot box?, 9. correct, 10. They who are here will vote.

page 16
1. left—action, 2. felt—linking, 3. made—action, 4. surprised—action, 5. attacked—action, 6. appeared—linking, 7. shot—action, 8. lived—action, 9. spoke—action, 10. entered—action, 11. heard—action, 12. was—linking, 13. became—linking, 14. graduated—action, 15. earned—action

page 17
1. may be **traveling**, 2. could **be**, 3. have been **held**, 4. were **thought**, 5. have **changed**, are **rearranging**, 6. could **result**, 7. will **protect**, 8. will **dive**, 9. should **keep**, 10.–13. Sentences will vary.

page 18
1. traveled—past, 2. had taken—past participle, 3. called—past, 4. are acting—present participle, 5. had worried—past participle, 6. shouted—past, 7. see—present, 8. are camping—present participle, 9. form—present, 10. caused—past, 11. are predicting—present participle, 12. walk, stop, hike, cry, arrive, 13. walking, stopping, hiking, crying, arriving, 14. walked, stopped, hiked, cried, arrived, 15. walked, stopped, hiked, cried, arrived

page 19
1. left—past participle, 2. found—past, 3. becoming—present participle, 4. shone—past, began—past, 5. burst—past, sprang—past, 6. ran—past, 7. put—past participle, 8. thought—past participle,

9. drunk—past participle, **10.** brought—past

page 20
1. fallen, blown, **2.** taken, **3.** given, **4.** gotten, forgotten,
5. written, grown, **6.** break, fly, wear, go, rise, **7.** breaking,
flying, wearing, going, rising, **8.** broke, flew, wore, went,
rose, **9.** broken, flown, worn, gone, risen, **10.** ran, run,
11. said, said, **12.** told, told, **13.** wrote, written. **14.** taught,
taught, **15.** swam, swum, **16.** built, built, **17.** spoke, spoken,
18. hid, hidden

page 21
1. don't, **2.** doesn't, **3.** hasn't, **4.** aren't, **5.** don't, **6.** isn't,
7. hasn't, **8.** don't, don't, **9.** was, **10.** are, **11.** has,
12. done, does

page 22
1. have been—present perfect, **2.** produced—past,
3. consider—present, **4.** have seen—present perfect, **5.** had
made—past perfect, **6.** came—past, **7.** meant—past, **8.** will
strike—future, **9.** wrestle—present, **10.** deposit—present,
11. will do—future, **12.** weaken—present, **13.** had
enrolled—past perfect, **14.** has changed—present perfect,
15. have found—present perfect, **16.** had thought—past
perfect, **17.** had appreciated—past perfect, **18.** have
created—present perfect, **19.** will have replaced—future
perfect, **20.** will have changed—future perfect

page 23
1. will give—gave, **2.** will strike—struck, **3.** used—use,
4. alternated—alternate, **5.** were—will be, **6.** was—is,
7. shared—will share, **8.** Had used—Will use,
9. made—makes, **10.** give—will give, **11.** have redefined,
12. had studied, **13.** have had, **14.** have appealed, **15.** will
have used

page 24
1. are, **2.** asked, expected, **3.** was, **4.** known, know,
expected, **5.** learned, became, became, became, **6.** started,
7. run, **8.** watched, **9.** waited, **10.** has, **11.** did, **12.** coached,
13. saw, **14.** If there had not been some embarrassing mix-
ups, I would have found relearning the language a painless
experience., **15.** After a while, I began to enjoy the lilting
way the voices of my British friends rose and fell.

page 25
1.–6. Sentences will vary. **1.** present progressive, **2.** past
perfect progressive, **3.** future progressive, **4.** present perfect
progressive, **5.** future perfect progressive, **6.** past
progressive, **7.** has been winning, **8.** had been baking,
9. was thinking, **10.** will be baking

page 26
1. Penguins/live/no direct object, **2.** Penguins/like/climate,
3. Penguins/use/wings, **4.** penguin/lays/egg,
5. penguin/tucks/this, **6.** penguins/return/no direct object,
7. you/Have read/books, **8.–10.** Sentences may vary.
8. Most people like these funny, tuxedoed birds and their
waddling walk., **9.** Sea World in San Diego, California,
built a climate-controlled ice island and a large icy pool for
the Emperor penguins., **10.** Most penguins eat small fish,
squid, and shrimp.

page 27
1. Visits/offer/people/views, **2.** Animals/can
bring/folk/enjoyment, **3.** Reserves and
refuges/afford/animals/protection,
4. reserves/offer/visitors/tours, **5.** Guidebooks and
programs/give/hikers/information, **6.** I/offered/dogs/treats,
7. I/gave/dog/warning, **8.** The university offered juniors
internships at a marine reserve., **9.** One reserve gave a
student a job observing the habits of sea lions.,
10. At the end of the semester, the student handed her
professor a fascinating report on the feeding of sea lions.,
11.–12. Sentences will vary.

page 28
1. link/drivers, **2.** work/requirement,
3. commitment/qualification, **4.** necessity/determination,
5. task/Controlling, **6.** tractors/vehicles, rigs/vehicles,
tankers/vehicles, **7.** enemy/weather, **8.** rain/conditions,
ice/conditions, heat/conditions, **9.** cause/Speeding,
10. lapse/cause, **11.** job/driving, **12.** diversion/it,
13. nightmares/Accidents, **14.** accidents/accidents,
15. puppy/Rinty, **16.** Corporal Lee Duncan/owner and
trainer, **17.** star/Rin Tin Tin, **18.** inspiration/She, **19.** jack-o-
lantern/pumpkin, **20.** squash/pumpkin

page 29
1. have traveled/intransitive,
2. have increased/knowledge/transitive,
3. brought/tales/transitive, **4.** have ventured/intransitive,
5. offer/expeditions/transitive, **6.** will lose/interest/transitive,
7. have traveled/intransitive, **8.** use/Coyote/transitive,
9. tricks/opponents/transitive, **10.** creates/world/transitive,
11. slays/monsters/transitive, **12.** backfire/intransitive,
13. have written/poems and stories/transitive

page 30
1. Young men and women have enjoyed surfing for many
years., **2.** Singing groups popularized the sport in many
parts of the country., **3.** Numerous groups played surfing
music., **4.** The music of these groups introduced many
teenagers to surfing., **5.** Many people still enjoy these
songs., **6.** Surfers all along the coast watch the waves
carefully., **7.** Surfers enjoy the exhilaration and sense of
freedom that come from riding the waves., **8.** Posters of
musicians cover the walls of the room., **9.** The Senate
approved a trade agreement with Mexico., **10.** They spent
most of their spare time on the farm.

page 31
1. lay, **2.** lying, **3.** left, **4.** let, **5.** set, **6.** sat, **7.** raised,
8. bring, **9.** sat, **10.** set, **11.** rise

page 32
1. adjectives: small, rough, articles: The, the, the, modified
words: boats, marina, water; **2.** adjective: seventy, article:
the, modified words: vessels, dock; **3.** adjectives: long,
small, gray, orange, articles: the, a, an, modified words:
dock, sloop, jib; **4.** adjective: large, proper adjective:
Australian, articles: A, the, a, modified words: team, sailors,
deck, schooner; **5.** adjectives: Some, enthusiastic, proper
adjective: Italian, articles: an, the, modified words: children,
tour, sailors; **6.** adjective: Wild, articles: a, the, modified
words: cheers, dinghy, channel; **7.** adjectives: old, heavy,

article: an, modified word: ferry; **8.** adjectives: dark, murky, articles: The, the, the, modified words: water, bottom, channel; **9.** adjective: fierce, article: a, modified word: wind; **10.** adjectives: large, busy, proper adjective: Indian, articles: A, the, modified words: city, coast; **11.** adjectives: fascinating, bustling, articles: The, a, modified words: city, seaport; **12.** adjectives: tropical, pleasant, warm, salty, article: The, modified words: climate, breezes; **13.** adjectives: colorful, crowded, article: the, modified words: scenes, streets; **14.** adjectives: financial, wealthy, proper adjectives: Indian, Middle Eastern article: the, modified words: exchange, merchants, traders

page 33
1. predicate adjective, predicate adjective, **2.** predicate nominative, **3.** predicate nominative, **4.** predicate adjective, **5.** predicate nominative, **6.** predicate adjective, **7.** predicate adjective, **8.** predicate adjective, **9.** predicate nominative, **10.** predicate adjective, **11.** predicate nominative, **12.** predicate nominative, **13.** predicate nominative, **14.** predicate adjective, **15.** predicate nominative, **16.** predicate adjective, **17.** predicate adjective, **18.** predicate adjective, predicate adjective, **19.** predicate adjective

page 34
1. tallest/superlative, **2.** taller/comparative, **3.** oldest/superlative, **4.** most important/superlative, **5.** most impressive/superlative, **6.** larger/comparative, **7.** Logging is the largest industry in Oregon., **8.** The loggers' organization is more powerful than many other groups., **9.** We are learning to be more careful of our forest than we once were., **10.** Unfortunately, the world's forests are smaller than they were even a few decades ago.

page 35
1. positive: Pacific, other; comparative: more populous, **2.** positive: Some; superlative: most beautiful, **3.** positive: hilly; superlative: most picturesque, **4.** positive: early, chilly; superlative: best, **5.** superlative: most important, **6.** positive: fabulous, **7.** positive: many; superlative: most useful, **8.** positive: two, great, spectacular, **9.** comparative: more crowded; superlative: Most, **10.** positive: Some, Mexican, Mexican, close, **11.** oldest, **12.** more beautiful, **13.** highest, **14.** more, **15.** busiest

page 36
1. best, **2.** less, **3.** fewer, **4.** worst, **5.** least, **6.** less, better, **7.** superlative, **8.** comparative, **9.** positive, **10.** comparative, **11.** positive, **12.** positive, **13.** comparative, **14.** superlative, **15.** comparative

page 37
1. best, **2.** bad, **3.** better, **4.** better, worse, **5.** more, **6.** best, **7.** best, **8.** better, more, **9.** worse, **10.** more, **11.** better, **12.** least, Reviews will vary.

page 38
1. adjective, **2.** pronoun, **3.** verb, **4.** adjective, **5.** adjective, **6.** verb, **7.** pronoun, **8.** adjective, **9.** adjective, **10.** pronoun, **11.** pronoun, **12.** adjective, **13.** verb, **14.** adjective, **15.** noun, **16.** adjective, **17.** adjective, **18.** pronoun, **19.** noun, **20.** adjective

page 39
1. High/live—verb, **2.** very/tenaciously—adverb, tenaciously/have clung—verb, **3.** extremely/interesting—adjective, **4.** frequently/visit—verb, **5.** most/famous—adjective, **6.** entirely/are based—verb, **7.** Never/are allowed—verb, **8.** brightly/colored—adjective, **9.** thoroughly/has been dried—verb, **10.** unusually/painstaking—adjective, **11.** Now/are made—verb, **12.–15.** Adverbs will vary.

page 40
1. farther, **2.** further, **3.** farthest, **4.** farther, **5.** further, **6.** high, **7.** highest, **8.** stealthily, **9.** most stealthily, **10.** more stealthily, **11.** most swiftly

page 41
1. barely, **2.** never, **3.** couldn't, **4.** wasn't, **5.** scarcely, **6.** not, **7.** ever, **8.** any, **9.** ever, **10.** no, **11.** any, **12.** ever, **13.** never, **14.** ever, **15.** no, **16.** anywhere

page 42
1. adverb, **2.** adverb, **3.** adjective, **4.** adjective, **5.** adverb, **6.** adjective, **7.** adverb, **8.** adjective, **9.** adverb, **10.** adverb, **11.** Almost, **12.** badly, **13.** well, **14.** really, **15.** good, Paragraphs will vary.

page 43
1. by the window/by, **2.** through his hair/through, in neat rows/in, across his desk/across, **3.** for the test/for, **4.** since Saturday afternoon/since, **5.** against his shirt/against, **6.** to himself/to, without confidence and concentration/without, **7.** out the smudged window/out, with a long face/with, **8.** with a sigh/with, on the first test question/on, **9.** into deep water/into, **10.** in a certain place/in, **11.** through binoculars/through, **12.** of the passengers/of, of a whale/of, **13.** to the right/to, **14.** in the group/in, **15.** of the moment/of, **16.** among the endangered species/among, **17.** for the world's whales/for, **18.** down the river/down, **19.** over the railing/over, **20.** for England/for, **21.** to the passengers/to

page 44
1. down the gangplank/down, **2.** into the Atlantic Ocean/into, **3.** for five days/for, **4.** For many people/For, **5.** of travel/of, **6.** in history/in, **7.** by the Chinese/by, **8.** without a rudder/without, **9.** by the stars/by, in clear weather/in, **10.** of the compass/of, in cloudy weather/in, **11.** in a book/in, in 1117/in, **12.** in China/in, at a much earlier date/at, **13.** of this invention/of, **14.** in our school/in, with the local museum/with, **15.** for everyone/for, **16.** At the museum's invitation/At, **17.** for the exhibition/for, at America/at, **18.** of our social studies department/of, into groups/into, **19.** in transportation/in, during the 1890s/during, **20.** of children/of, in the late nineteenth century/in, **21.** of students/of, on the growing interest/on, in photography/in, **22.** for the arts/for, in America/in, **23.** for each major theme/for, in the show/in, **24.** about the world's fair/about, in Chicago/in, in 1893/in, **25.** of the great Ferris wheel/of, by George W. Gale Ferris/by, **26.** of the attractions/of, at the fair/at, **27.** to Chicago/to, from many countries/from, **28.** of the 1890s/of, **29.** In the late nineteenth century/In, for children's toys/for, **30.** with alphabet blocks/with

136

page 45

1. for a thousand years—adverb phrase, may have been growing, 2. near the water's surface—adjective phrase, Coral, 3. on live coral—adverb phrase, settles, 4. by ignorant or irresponsible divers—adverb phrase, are destroyed, 5. to a coral reef—adjective phrase, damage, 6. against coral formations—adverb phrase, should brush, 7. on the coral—adverb phrase, should lie or sit, 8. of dead or damaged coral—adjective phrase, cost, 9. at many popular diving destinations—adjective phrase, guides, 10. under the sea—adjective phrase, resources

page 46

1. of birds—adjective phrase, migrations; in nature—adjective phrase, events, 2. of migrating birds—adjective phrase, species; of miles—adjective phrase, thousands, 3. of the Arctic tern—adjective phrase, journey, 4. from the far North—adverb phrase, flies; to Antarctica—adverb phrase, flies, 5. of approximately 9,000 miles—adjective phrase, distance, 6. at night—adverb phrase, migrate; for long distances—adverb phrase, travel; across the open ocean—adverb phrase, travel, 7. to their destinations—adjective phrase, way, 8. about bird navigation—adjective phrase, theories, 9. to the earth's magnetic field—adverb phrase, sensitive, 10. for reference points—adverb phrase, use; in their long flights—adverb phrase, use, 11. for the birds' migration—adjective phrase, reason; for food—adjective phrase, need, 12. in northern climates—adverb phrase, begins; for many species—adverb phrase, scarce, 13. in warmer areas—adverb phrase, plentiful, 14. in summer—adverb phrase, fly, 15. in northern latitudes—adjective phrase, days; for birds—adjective phrase, advantage

page 47

1. Lupe visited her aunt in Guatemala., 2. Besides wanting to see a new country, Lupe wanted her aunt to teach her how to weave., 3. Lupe's aunt was among the best weavers in her town., 4. Lupe knew her training at her aunt's would require much work., 5. Lupe's first trip into town from her aunt's country house was overwhelming., 6. Artisans displaying their wares crowded beside food stalls and animal vendors., 7. She couldn't believe so much could be happening in one place., 8. After Lupe had been at the market some time, she became hungry., 9. She stood between two food stalls, trying to decide what to buy to eat., 10. Lupe remembered she had several juice drinks in her backpack.

page 48

1. sentence, 2. sentence, 3. not a sentence, 4. sentence. 5. sentence, 6. sentence, 7. sentence, 8. not a sentence. 9. sentence, 10. not a sentence, 11. not a sentence, 12. sentence, 13. not a sentence, 14. sentence, 15. not a sentence

page 49

1. question mark/interrogative, 2. exclamation point/exclamatory, 3. period/imperative, 4. question mark/interrogative, 5. period/declarative, 6. exclamation point/exclamatory, 7. question mark/interrogative, 8. period/imperative, 9. question mark/interrogative, 10. exclamation point/exclamatory, 11. If you ever get a chance, stop and watch a mime., 12. They like to imitate you behind your back., 13. My goodness, there's one now!., 14. Fiddler crabs appear at low tide., 15. Look at the pincers on the male crabs! (.), 16. How unusual they are!., 17. Can you see why they are called fiddler crabs?., 18. What do they use the pincers for?., 19. The crabs use them to signal to females and to protect their territory., 20. They are small, but they look very fierce.

page 50

1. Many framers of the United States Constitution/framers, 2. Certain basic rights/rights, 3. The initial document/document, 4. Some states/states, 5. People/People, 6. A group of men calling themselves the Federalists/group, 7. Madison/Madison, 8. The first ten amendments to the Constitution/amendments, 9. They/They, 10. (You)/(You), 11. The Bill of Rights/Bill of Rights, 12. My brothers/brothers, 13. (You)/(You), 14. The contents of that letter/contents, 15. Two classmates of mine/classmates, 16. This secret/secret, 17. The secret/secret, 18. My relatives/relatives, 19. Even Aunt Maria/Aunt Maria, 20. I/I

page 51

1. invited six girls to an unusual birthday party/invited, 2. met at a stable in the desert/met, 3. had rented eight horses, one for each girl and one for herself/had rented, 4. had been packed into each of the eight saddle bags/had been packed, 5. were given the most docile horses/were given, 6. had any real trouble getting to the lunch spot/had, 7. returned to the stable after a brief rest and an investigation of the desert landscape/returned, 8. is Sydney/is, 9. is a major port in southeastern Australia/is, 10. pass through the port/pass, 11. include wool, wheat, and meat/include, 12. is spectacular/is, 13. is a modern opera house/is, 14. spans Port Jackson gracefully with a single steel arch/spans, 15. is a popular recreation area/is, 16. admire Australia's unusual animals/admire, 17. delights most viewers/delights, 18. is one of Australia's most unusual animals/is, 19. have probably seen pictures of koalas and kangaroos/have seen, 20. are found nowhere else in the world/are found

page 52

Sentences will vary.

page 53

1. compound subject—Ms. Ramírez, Mr. Singh, 2. compound predicate—gives, donates, 3. compound predicate—manages, plays, 4. compound predicate—plays, acts, 5. compound predicate—plans, conducts, 6. compound subject—musicians, ushers, 7. compound predicate—gather, practice, 8. compound predicate—clap, cheer, 9. compound subject—symphony, concerto, 10. compound predicate—has toured, has appeared, 11. compound subject—Clarinetists, flutists, oboists, 12. compound subject—harp, piano, 13. compound predicate—vary, enrich, 14. compound subject—Felicia, Alfio, 15. compound predicate—came, joined, 16. compound subject—girl, brother, 17. compound predicate—enjoyed, were, 18. compound subject—mother, father, 19. compound subject—Alfio, Felicia, 20. compound predicate—understood, had discussed, 21. compound predicate—lived, visited, 22. compound predicate—talked, kept, 23. compound subject—Felicia, Alfio, 24. compound predicate—rushed, ran, 25. compound predicate—was fixing, wished

page 54

Sentences will vary. Suggested: **1.** Bicycles and feet take you in and out of small hamlets; they put you in contact with everyday life., **2.** People living in the countryside see fewer tourists, and they are often eager to talk to foreigners., **3.** You may be able to learn the local language, or some of the local people may speak English., **4.** Denzel's father agreed to help him, and the two of them took a drive on a calm, sunny day., **5.** Denzel held his wind gauge upright outside the car window; the open notch on the gauge faced into the wind., **6.** The air entered the wind gauge, and the pressure lifted the plastic foam ball., **7.** Denzel's father told him the car's speed, and Denzel marked it on the cardboard.

page 55

1. simple subjects: Traveling, it; verbs: may be, is; compound, **2.** simple subject: you; verbs: Have considered; simple, **3.** simple subject: Trains; verbs: take, speed, bypass; simple, **4.** simple subject: Traveler; verb: experience; simple, **5.** simple subject: you; verb: Have seen; simple, **6.** simple subject: hole; verb: measures; simple, **7.** simple subjects: meteorite, it; verbs: crashed, may have fallen; compound, **8.** simple subjects: meteorite, people; verbs: streaked, could see; compound, **9.** simple subject: it; verb: Did weigh; simple, **10.** simple subjects: meteorite, it; verbs: exploded, created; compound, **11.** simple subjects: Denzel, he; verbs: was interested, decided; compound, **12.** simple subject: Denzel; verb: made; simple, **13.** simple subject: he; verb: made; simple, **14.** simple subjects: He, he; verbs: cut, plugged; compound, **15.** simple subject: Denzel; verb: cut; simple, **16.** simple subjects: Denzel, he; verbs: put, pinned; compound, **17.** simple subjects: He, he; verbs: dropped, pinned; compound, **18.** simple subject: Denzel; verb: held; simple, **19.** simple subjects: He, he; verbs: had finished, needed; compound, **20.** simple subjects: Denzel, he; verbs: had, asked; compound

page 56

1. Both, and—correlative, **2.** and—coordinating, **3.** but—coordinating, **4.** both, and—correlative, **5.** but—coordinating, **6.** Either, or—correlative, **7.** Just, so—correlative, **8.** but—coordinating, **9.** or—coordinating. Paragraphs will vary.

page 57

1.–10. Interjections will vary., **11.** Hey! Who do you think could have left that shoe here?, **12.** Oh, just ask Kim; she's the school detective., **13.** Ah, this will be an easy case to solve., **14.** Impossible! How can you tell whose shoe this is?, **15.** Well, do you notice that the shoelaces are green?, **16.** Gee, doesn't Mark wear sneakers with green laces?

page 58

Sentences will vary. Suggested: **1.** Games have been around for thousands of years. In Egypt alone at least four games were played as early as 2700 B.C., **2.** Archaeologists and historians sometimes have to reconstruct game rules for ancient games., **3.** Clay pieces found in burial sites and notes written on papyrus can help historians reconstruct game rules., **4.** New games are being created all the time; only some will stand the test of time., **5.** High on the mesas north and west of Chaco were other ruins that looked similar. Could they have been part of Chaco?

page 59

Sentences will vary. Suggested:

MANDY: Who wouldn't want to go to the end-of-the-year party?
SARA: Jeffrey doesn't if they aren't going to have live music.
MANDY: What does that matter? I suppose hearing live music is the only thing that matters?
SARA: It is to some people. It is to Jeff and his best friend, Mike.
MANDY: Who cares what they think? They wouldn't know good music if their lives depended on it.
SARA: I know! I can't believe that would actually stop them from going.
MANDY: Well, the party will be much more fun without them if they are going to make such a fuss.
SARA: You're right but they are such fun! Jessica thinks the party will be boring without them.
MANDY: I have an idea. Why not let Jeff and Mike act as disc jockeys? That way they can play the music most people like.
SARA: Wow, that is a great idea!

page 60

Sentences will vary. Suggested: **1.** Mr. Escudero, a strong supporter of public television, decided to have his eighth-grade class debate the merits of TV., **2.** He divided the class into pro-TV and anti-TV factions and supplied the students with research materials., **3.** The students searched books and magazines for supporting facts and organized their arguments., **4.** Mr. Escudero and some of the students began to believe that they should have limited the scope of the debate to commercial TV., **5.** Some of the books and magazines pointed out the differences in programming between commercial and public TV., **6.** Portuguese explorers, the first Europeans to see Madagascar, landed there around 1500.

page 61

1. independent, **2.** independent, **3.** subordinate, **4.** subordinate, **5.** subordinate, **6.** subordinate, **7.** subordinate, **8.** independent, **9.** subordinate, **10.** subordinate, **11.** subordinate, **12.** subordinate, **13.** independent, **14.** subordinate, **15.** independent, **16.** subordinate, **17.** subordinate, **18.** independent, **19.** independent, **20.** subordinate

page 62

1.–10. Sentences will vary. Be sure that each sentence contains a subordinate clause.

page 63

1. who was a famous singer/who—nonrestrictive, **2.** that featured blues and jazz bands/that—restrictive, **3.** that was known as the home of the blues/that—restrictive, **4.** who were other well-known performers/who—nonrestrictive, **5.** whose music never goes out of style/whose—restrictive, **6.** that she enjoyed/that—restrictive, **7.** that gave her much satisfaction/that—restrictive, **8.** which was still young for Alberta Hunter/which—nonrestrictive, **9.** Jazz is a form of music that has many styles., **10.** Swing, which was popularized in the 1940s, is a style of jazz.

page 64
1. <u>when</u> he was still a teenager, 2. <u>Although</u> Adams was also an avid conservationist, 3. <u>as if</u> they are from another world, 4. <u>Since</u> Adams died, 5. <u>Though</u> many have studied his technique, 6. <u>because</u> every girl did her share of the work, 7. <u>While</u> you were at school, 8. Photographing animals is difficult because they are unpredictable., 9. Keisha used a telephoto lens so she wouldn't startle the heron., 10. I prefer taking underwater pictures because the water makes photography more challenging.

page 65
1. that the mail had come—direct object, 2. that a letter had come for me—direct object, 3. What he handed me—subject, 4. that it was made from a brown paper bag—predicate nominative, 5. if the sender was very young—direct object, 6. why I thought so—direct object, 7. Whoever addressed this letter—subject, 8. how it was written—object of a preposition, 9. who had sent it—direct object, 10. That I had been invited to the party—subject, 11. who else would be there—predicate nominative, 12. whoever comes to that funny party—object of a preposition, 13. What you say—subject, 14. what you make it—predicate nominative, 15. where the rainbow began—direct object, 16.–20. Sentences will vary.

page 66
1. Propelled by dreams of great riches—explorers, 2. farming—country, 3. grazing—land, 4. Flushed with visions of gold-encrusted hills—adventurers, 5. concerning land claims—fights, 6. battling—land-grabbers, 7. Determined to guard their patches of land—miners, 8. flowing—river, 9. seeping from the earth—oil, 10. thriving—attractions, 11. Arriving in tour buses—people, 12. elected by the class—student, 13. barking—dogs

page 67
1. beginning, 2. dancing with amateur groups, 3. leaping like a gazelle, 4. Leaving Moscow, 5. praising his performances, 6. cheering, 7. Watching his impossibly high leaps, 8. dancing, 9. Driving in a crowded city, 10. humming that tune, 11. gerund—subject, 12. gerund phrase—object of a preposition, 13. gerund phrase—subject, 14. gerund—predicate nominative, 15. gerund phrase—direct object, 16. gerund phrase—direct object, 17. gerund phrase—object of a preposition, 18. gerund phrase—subject

page 68
1. to protect their rights—noun, 2. to protest taxation without representation—adverb, 3. To protect their comfortable position—adverb, 4. to succeed in their revolt—adverb, 5. to become educated—adjective, 6. to vote—noun, 7. to grade today—adverb, 8. to see the manager—noun, 9. to start—adverb, 10. Civil libertarians took to the streets and the courts to achieve their goal., 11. They fought for the rights of all Americans to vote., 12. Now each American has a responsibility to exercise that right to vote.

page 69
1. to gain—split infinitive, 2. Considering and reconsidering every word—dangling participle, 3. to select—split infinitive, 4. Writing at least two paragraphs every day for the past year—correct, 5. Hovering over his journal—dangling participle, 6. to leap—split infinitive, 7. Shaking his head uncertainly—correct, 8. to find—split infinitive, 9. to write—split infinitive, 10. Carrying his journal and his application form—correct, 11. to speak, to tell—correct, 12. hearing the raging river—correct

page 70
Sentences will vary. Suggested: 1. Having pucks shot at you at 120 miles an hour is not fun., 2. correct, 3. On the ice a goalie must always concentrate on the puck., 4. To stop the puck, you must ignore everything but the game., 5. A goalie wouldn't last very long on the rink without protective gear., 6. To fans sitting forty feet away from the ice, hockey seems grueling., 7. A baseball scout from the Brooklyn Dodgers spotted him when the young player was eighteen., 8. correct, 9. One merchant brought sapphires from Burma., 10. He displayed them only to jewelers., 11. The large sapphire was sold just that day.

page 71
Students should capitalize the first letter of each of the words given. 1. On—., 2. How—!, 3. The—., 4. The—., 5. Have—?, 6. The—!, 7. Listen! You—!, 8. I—., 9. Have—?, 10. Have—?, 11. What—!, 12. Think—., 13. Do—?, 14. The—., 15. How—!, 16. Can—?, 17. Look—., 18. Do—?, 19. How—!, 20. Is—?, 21. No—., 22. Wow—!, 23. There—., 24. Have—?, 25. No—., 26. I—., 27. Has—?, 28. Look—., 29. What—!, 30. What—!

page 72
1. We will visit the Louvre when we go to France this spring., 2. Julian, my brother, is the only one in our family who can speak French., 3. Julian can speak French, Spanish, and Japanese., 4. We had an exchange student from Madrid at our house last year, and he and Julian became good friends., 5. The *Jeu de Pomme*, which features Impressionist artists, is definitely my favorite museum., 6. Besides having lovely paintings, the museum stands in a beautiful park., 7. No, I have never traveled to France., 8. Dan, it takes courage to stand up for your rights.

page 73
1. The river rafters huddled under a tree; it had been raining steadily for an hour., 2. They had met at the Pancake House at 7:30 that morning., 3. The two big rafts lay in a muddy puddle of water, and the provisions (food, water, extra paddles, and sleeping bags) were piled under a tarp., 4. One man looked glumly at the planned itinerary: Roseville, Salamander Island, and Bishop's Gate., 5. If this trip were canceled—and it looked as if it would be—everyone would be disappointed., 6. The recipe called for one-half cup of sugar and one-fourth cup of flour.,

page 74
1. thirty, 2. twelve, fifteen, 3. Two thousand, 4. sixty, 5. 1930s, 6. 1, 7. two hundred, 8. 16, 9. 800, 10. Twenty, 11. 100,000, 12. 8, 13. Cape Cod lies 250 miles to the north., 14. This weekend 106 sailboats will race to the Cape., 15. Coming from as far as the Caribbean, 532 crew members will take part in the race.

page 75

Capitalize or lowercase the first letter of each of the following words. **1.** multinational, explorers, North Pole, Tuesday, **2.** friend, Captain Wilkins, Arctic Circle, explorers, ship, **3.** ship, Senator, United Nations, English, Russian, French, Chinese, **4.** ship, Golden Gate Bridge, I, good-bye, friend, **5.** ship, explorers, north, dogsleds, Canada, **6.** Mr., Ming's, **7.** Greek Parthenon, Athens, architectural, **8.** Roman, architects, Greeks, **9.** Romans, Etruscans, Asians, semicircular, **10.** Grecian, **11.** Sen., **12.** South American, **13.** AK, **14.** Italian, **15.** Canadian

page 76

1. United States of America, **2.** United Nations, **3.** North Atlantic Treaty Organization, **4.** tablespoon, **5.** teaspoon, **6.** Company, **7.** Mister, **8.** vice president, **9.** Captain, **10.** Missouri, **11.** pound, **12.** miles per hour, **13.** ml, **14.** M. S., **15.** Ave., **16.** kg, **17.** Cir., **18.** oz., **19.** NJ, **20.** Dr., **21.** Inc., **22.** Jr., **23.** yd., **24.** mg, **25.** l, **26.** cc, **27.** Blvd., **28.** Rd., **29.** NCAA, **30.** rpm, **31.** F, **32.** C, **33.** NY, **34.** Sun.

page 77

36 Oakly Road
Hornell, New York 14802
October 5, 2003

Dear Janet,

College is such a new experience! It's taken me a month to get used to all the new routines. It's also a little scary. Sometimes I miss being home.

Write soon and tell me all about Ridge High. I'll see you at Thanksgiving.

Regards,
Angie

page 78

1. I read an article in Esquire magazine yesterday., **2.** It was titled "Senior Prom Revisited.", **3.** The writer is a well-known reporter for The Sacramento Bee., **4.** The article contained an excerpt from the book Going Home Again., **5.** Everyone was curious about a sculpture called Locker that stood in the gymnasium., **6.** One man brought a video crew from the television program You Are There., **7.** Where is last week's issue of Time?, **8.** Have you read John Steinbeck's book Travels With Charley?, **9.** I just found that article, "Welcome to Pittsburgh.", **10.** Have you seen the movie Beauty and the Beast?, **11.** My family enjoys watching Monday Night Football.

page 79

1. Scott asked Melanie why she wasn't at the television workshop that morning., **2.** "I went on an audition instead," she answered., **3.** "Tell me all about it. Was it a play or a commercial?" asked Scott., **4.** Melanie answered by handing Scott the script., **5.** Girl (Reading a book while riding a skateboard): Who said bookworms are square? Announcer: January is National Library Month. Escape with a book!, **6.** "Wow!" Scott yelled as he read the script. "A commercial!"

page 80

1. Jerome, once a thriving copper-mining town, sits on the edge of Mingus Mountain in Arizona.—Jerome, **2.** When the mine closed, Jerome became a ghost town, a town without people.—town, **3.** It remained that way for many years, until artists, potters, and weavers, people seeking a quiet lifestyle, rediscovered Jerome.—artists, potters, weavers, **4.** Now the company, "Made in Jerome," makes handsome pottery there.—company, **5.** Local cottage industries, small home-based businesses, sell arts and crafts.—industries, **6.** From Prescott you can get to Jerome by driving over Mingus Mountain, a 7,743-foot peak.—Mingus Mountain, **7.** Madagascar, the world's fourth-largest island, lies off the coast of Africa in the Indian Ocean.—Madagascar, **8.** Portuguese explorers, the first Europeans to see Madagascar, landed there around 1500.—explorers, **9.** Tom Brokaw, an anchor on the evening news, has retired.—Tom, **10.** Two of my classes, algebra and marketing, were canceled today.—classes

page 81

1. beach, **2.** sword, **3.** pain, **4.** reel, faint, **5.** manner, air, **6.** flair, **7.** sleight, **8.** shone, **9.** principal, **10.** rye, **11.–14.** Sentences will vary.

page 82

1. intercollegiate, **2.** disqualified, misplaced, **3.** Dejected, **4.** disappointed, overlooked, **5.–8.** Prefixes, words, and sentences will vary.

page 83

1. ive—thorough, complete, **2.** tion—the state of being deprived; able—easily irritated, **3.** less, ness—the state of being without rest, **4.** able—capable of being measured, **5.–8.** Words and sentences will vary.

page 84

1.–5. Answers will vary. Suggested: **1.** Mrs. Stamper had a lot of things going on at once., **2.** She had told so many people about the party that she felt she had repeated the same words over and over again., **3.** She gave all the guests a signal to sneak into the basement., **4.** Mark was very happy when everyone yelled, "Surprise!", **5.** Albert was in trouble, so he did not go to the party., **6.** the runaround, **7.** raining cats and dogs, **8.** run rings around, **9.** down in the dumps, **10.** off the wall, **11.** in the same boat, **12.** walking on air, **13.** in hot water, **14.** fly off the handle, **15.** put our heads together

page 85

1. write, **2.** find, **3.** works, **4.** says, **5.** talks, **6.** send, **7.** seems, **8.** cries, **9.** are, **10.** has, **11.** have, **12.** does, **13.** hear, **14.** has, **15.** orbit, **16.** boxes, **17.** is, **18.** are, **19.** flashes, **20.** hangs, **21.** read, **22.** hurry, **23.** creates, **24.** does, **25.** drives, **26.** drive, **27.** eats, **28.** teaches, **29.** paint, **30.** walk

page 86

1. The telephone's piercing ring wrenched me awake yet again. I clambered out of bed for the third time that evening. I was so angry that I almost shouted. "Hello, Hello!" I screamed into the phone. Getting no answer, I jerked the receiver from my ear and stared at it, as if it could tell me who was on the other end. Disgusted, I slammed down the receiver. Whoever was calling and leaving me with silence would get a deafening whistle blast the next time my sleep was disturbed., **2.** Angry: The writer is awakened from sleep. The writer almost shouts. The writer screams into the phone. The writer is frustrated that no one is answering, looks at the receiver for an answer, and gets none. The writer is disgusted and slams down the receiver., **3.** Accept reasonable responses that add to the story sequentially and use first-person point of view.

page 87

1. Who?—I, Kate O'Reilly; What?—Kate tries to catch a baseball and ends up in a hospital room.; Where?—first a baseball field, then a hospital room; Why?—She gets hit with the baseball.; How?—This is not stated, but it is implied that she missed the ball., 2. Sight—an explosion of light, white walls and sheets, everything dark; Hearing—the crack of the bat, a low-pitched moaning, Touch—swirling in a tunnel, pillow felt like rocks

page 88

Errors are corrected in bold type.

(indent paragraph) I stood nervously at the water's edge with the rest of the racers. I checked and rechecked my suit and goggles. I stared across the lake, hoping to sight some secret about the race. I can remember now that I was shivering, but I had no sensation of cold. We were all **too** scared to be cold. The crowd seemed **noisy**, restless. Then suddenly everyone was still.

(indent paragraph) At the sound of the gun there was pandemonium. The water churned with elbows, knees, and **feet**. I felt as if **I** were drowning. I couldn't catch my breath. I actually began to think of hanging back. **Perhaps** I should wait for the others to take the lead and then try to catch up. Suddenly, one of my old swimming **rivals** passed me.

(indent paragraph) Galvanized, I set my **course** for the finish line. The familiar sound of water whooshing **past** my ears was reassuring. I found my rhythm and settled into it. Breathe, kick, stroke; breathe, kick, stroke. **Don't** think about it; just keep going. Now all that mattered was passing **was passing (delete)** the swimmers in front of me.

I felt **like I** must have been swimming for hours. I became disoriented, for I could see no one around me. Had the other swimmers left me so far behind**?** Had I strayed into the wrong part of the lake? Still I continued breathing, kicking, stroking, trying not to think. I could hear a distant roaring. I only kept swimming; I had become a robot. When my stomach scraped sand, I stood up shakily. The roaring became cheering, and I **knew** I had won the race.

page 89

Writing plans will vary.

page 90

First drafts will vary.

page 91

1. how to clean mildew off painted surfaces; 2. 1)Mix laundry bleach with water. 2) Add powdered cleanser. 3) Scrub the mixture onto the surface. 4) Allow the mixture to dry. 5) Rinse off the mixture.; 3. one cup of laundry bleach, two quarts of water, two tablespoons of powdered cleanser, a toothbrush or scrub brush, rinse water; 4. A pail or other container would be needed for mixing the ingredients for cleaning.; 5. Fight mildew as soon as you discover it. Since it is a growth, you must kill the molds that cause mildew or it will grow back. You can repaint the surface when it is completely dry.

page 92

1. U—This is not related to the topic., 2. E, 3. U— This is not a step in preparation for diving., 4. E, 5. E, 6. U—This detail is not a step in preparedness for diving., 7. E, 8. U—This information interrupts the flow of the how-to., 9. E, 10. E, 11. U—This detail in not related to the topic.

page 93

Errors are corrected in bold type.

How often during the day do you feel tense**?** Do the stresses of being a student, a friend, a son or a **daughter**, an athlete**,** or a musician sometimes seem too much for you? **You** probably need to take a few minutes and relax**.** Using specific relaxation techniques can help you.

In order to learn relaxation techniques, you need only a quiet room and a **comfortable** place to sit or recline. Before you settle yourself, you may want to darken the room slightly.

Begin by closing your eyes and breathing deeply, in through your nose and out **through** your mouth. **Do** this three or four times**. Feel** your breath entering your body. Then imagine your breath traveling through all your muscles, relaxing them. Imagine that you are lying on a warm beach or in a fragrant meadow. As you continue breathing, think of each part of **your** body relaxing. Notice how heavy your legs are becoming. Feel each vertebra in your spine loosen and relax**.** Feel the knots in your shoulders loosen, and imagine a soft **summer** breeze blowing through your hair. You may even begin to feel as if you are floating. This means you are achieving **relaxation**.

(indent paragraph) **Try** this technique every time you feel tense. Relaxation exercises can help you perform your everyday tasks a bit more productively and can help you feel refreshed.

page 94

Writing plans will vary.

page 95

First drafts will vary.

page 96

Topic sentence: The wastelands of Antarctica and the Sahara in Africa are entirely different kinds of deserts., 1. This is a paragraph of contrast. The words *different* and *in contrast* signal that the paragraph is one of contrast., 2. The detail sentences are arranged in the subject-by-subject method., Topic sentence: Singers and athletes have much in common., 3. This is a paragraph of comparison. The words *much in common*, *in the same way*, and *too* signal a paragraph of comparison., 4. The detail sentences are arranged in the feature-by-feature method.

page 97

Answers will vary. 1. Both make tedious tasks easier., 2. Both are continents., 3. Both transport people or cargo., 4. Both provide warmth., 5.–6. Answers will vary.

page 98

Errors are corrected in bold type.

Although the rococo style of art and architecture developed out of the baroque style, the two were quite different**. The** baroque style developed in **Europe**, England, and Latin America during the sixteenth and seventeenth centuries. Its essential design characteristics **. (delete) were** based on a grand scale. Words such as *drama* and *energy* are often used to describe paintings and buildings in the baroque style**. Examples** of baroque architecture include Versailles in Paris and Christopher Wren's churches in England. Some of the European churches and monuments built in the baroque style are **almost** overwhelming in their multitude of forms. Rococo is usually considered **. (delete)** a much more relaxed and intimate style than baroque. In contrast with the heavy grandness of baroque, the rococo style is more refined and delicate. Designs using shells, scrolls, branches**,** and flowers appeared on furniture, tapestries, and sculptures throughout eighteenth century Europe**. Rococo** artists also used elements of Oriental art in their designs. Many of the palaces and churches still standing in southern Germany and **Austria** present outstanding examples of the rococo style**. Another** fine example can be seen in the furniture of Thomas Chippendale from **London.**

page 99
Writing plans will vary.

page 100
First drafts will vary.

page 101
Topic sentence: Dara yawned all through first and second periods and fell asleep at her desk in chemistry today., **1.** It is an effect., **2.** Dara baby-sat on Saturday night until midnight. She read for a while when she got home. On Sunday she washed and waxed the car, played soccer, and studied until 10 P.M. These sentences are causes., Topic sentence: The sirocco is a hot, steady wind that blows from the Libyan deserts., **3.** It is a cause., **4.** It is a familiar but dreaded yearly occurrence. This oppressive wind brings dust and rain across the Mediterranean. Tempers grow short, and some people become ill. These sentences are effects., **5.** Sentences will vary. Accept all sentences in which students give a cause sentence for the effect topic sentence or an effect sentence for the cause topic sentence.

page 102
Answers will vary. Suggested: **1.** top box: improving your posture; bottom boxes: clothes fit better, better lung capacity; Sentence: If you improve your posture, your clothes fit better and you have better lung capacity., **2.** top box: have more energy; bottom boxes: eat whole grains, get more sleep; Sentence: You'll have more energy if you eat whole grains and get more sleep., **3.** second box: less appetite, eat less; third box: lose weight, clothes fit; Sentence: As you exercise more, you'll gain self-confidence because you'll eat less and look trimmer and your clothes will fit better.

page 103
Errors are corrected in bold type.
The death of body tissues from a lack of oxygen **is** called gangrene. There **are** three distinct types of gangrene, each with a specific cause.
(indent paragraph) The most common form of this disorder is dry gangrene, which is caused by a gradual loss of blood supply. As the blood supply **diminishes**, the body tissues fail to receive crucial nutrients. Unless the process of loss is reversed, the tissue slowly **dies**. Dry gangrene may be the result of an illness such as diabetes or arteriosclerosis. It may also result from frostbite, which is caused by **exposure** to cold. The hands, feet, ears, and nose **are** the body parts most often affected.
Moist gangrene is a much more serious condition. It **is** caused by a sudden loss of blood supply to part of the body**.** This sudden loss is typically the result of a wound or burn. Certain kinds of blood clots may also cause a sudden

loss of blood and **result** in moist gangrene. The affected body part becomes infected, and the **infection** may spread **spread (delete)** to other parts of the body.
The third form of gangrene, now rather uncommon, **is** especially dangerous. Gas gangrene is caused by specific bacteria within a wound. Gas gangrene must be treated as soon as possible; untreated gas gangrene can cause death within a few days.

page 104
Writing plans will vary.

page 105
First drafts will vary.

page 106
1. Construction of Interstate 3 should begin immediately to divert trucks from already-clogged local streets., **2.** The bicycle helmet law now in effect is the sanest law the state has passed this year., **3.** An alternative means of netting must be instituted to save protected species., **4.** Supporting argument, **5.** Introduction, **6.** Supporting argument, **7.** Conclusion, **8.–9.** Answers may vary but should be supported with logical reasons. Suggested: **8.** Many of our cities, even our smaller ones, are being choked by pollution., **9.** Number 6. It is the less important of the two given. The second argument strengthens the first one.

page 107
1. fact, **2.** fact, **3.** opinion, **4.** fact, **5.** fact, **6.** opinion, **7.** opinion, **8.** Answers will vary.

page 108
Errors are corrected in bold type.
(indent paragraph) The Saturday recreation program at **Salisbury** School should be reinstated. This program was clearly one of the **most** successful in the **school's** history. Of all the recreation classes, the gymnastics classes were **most** popular. However, the other classes, especially those in art, dance, volleyball, and soccer, were also consistently popular. The number of students who wanted to enroll was often **greater** than the number of spaces available. Children of all ages looked forward to participating in these recreation activities. In addition, they enjoyed the **opportunity** of spending **Saturdays** with their friends and of making new friends in the recreation classes. An additional advantage was that no one was excluded; supplies were always provided for those who could not afford to **buy** their own class materials**.** These program advantages make one wonder why the Saturday recreation hours were discontinued at all.
(indent paragraph) It is clear that many people in the **community** support reinstatement of the recreation program. Some have launched a donation drive to provide the school with **much needed** uniforms and equipment. Others have offered **their** own time to supervise the general activities in the recreation area and to free the staff for teaching duties. Parents, educators, and children all agree that closing the recreation program has deprived members of the West Ridge community of valuable activities. Working toward the good of the **community** is **more** important than trying to save a little money.

page 109
Writing plans will vary.

page 110
First drafts will vary.

page 111
1. Sensory details: mountainous bulk, radio droning, buzz saw, shrieking, boomed, pungent smell of garlic, **2.** sight—mountainous bulk., sound—droning radio, buzz saw, shrieking, boomed., smell—pungent smell of garlic, **3.** mountainous bulk—metaphor, The Sleeping Giant—metaphor, snored like a buzz saw—simile, shrieking like a gaggle of alarmed geese—simile, slept like a stone—simile, **4.** Answers will vary.

page 112
1. voice : reverberated as bass drum : booming, **2.** gait : stumpy as dwarfs : short-legged, **3.** crown : gleamed as billiard bass : shiny, **4.** dogs : skittered as frightened rabbits : running, **5.–10.** Analogies will vary.

page 113
Errors are corrected in bold type.

At first glance, Natalie seems as graceful as a stork picking through weeds for food. **Her** thin arms and sinewy legs jut awkwardly when **she** walks. Like a bird, however, Natalie is **at (delete)** more at home in the air, and when she dances she rarely remains on the ground for long. As she dances, Natalie becomes a soaring gull; her earthbound friends are left to stare up at **her** enviously.

Beneath **Natalie's** seemingly **fragile** airborne beauty is an iron will. Practicing doggedly for hours, she bends and stretches; her muscles are bundles of **effort**. The partner with **whom** she has been dancing for years is a wrung-out rag halfway through a typical practice session.

Natalie rarely talks about dancing; she prefers to practice or perform. After repeatedly refusing to answer my questions about **her** dancing, Natalie finally invited me to visit a private class that she and her partner had scheduled. I watched as **they** spent hours revising and polishing, working and reworking. **Haggard** with effort and disappointed with their progress, **she** slumped against the wall until she got a second wind. Natalie insisted that they keep working until each movement was right.

Two weeks after that class, **I** saw their first performance of the finished dance. All sense of effort, every hint of work, had disappeared. Natalie seemed to be a comet streaking across the stage.

page 114
Writing plans will vary.

page 115
First drafts will vary.

page 116
Answers will vary. Suggested: **1.** No. This is unsuitable because it is too personal; it is more like an autobiography or a biography topic., **2.** Yes, **3.** Yes, **4.** No. This is not an objective topic for a research paper., **5.** Yes., **6.** Sentences will vary. Body statements should add one or more details about the topic. Conclusions should be summary statements.

page 117
1. Summaries will vary. Suggested: The Enlightenment of the 18th century, also known as the Age of Reason, was a time of great scientific and intellectual growth. The Age of Reason grew out of the belief in natural law and universal order espoused by great thinkers of the 17th century. Benjamin Franklin and Thomas Jefferson are famous Age of Reason thinkers., **2.** Answers will vary. Suggested: The Enlightenment of the 18th century, also known as the Age of Reason, was a time of great scientific and intellectual growth., **3.** Answers will vary. Suggested: It grew out of the belief in natural law and universal order. Benjamin Franklin and Thomas Jefferson were Age of Reason thinkers.

page 118
Errors are corrected in bold type.

Asteroids, also called minor planets or planetoids, were first discovered in the early nineteenth century. They are small, irregularly shaped bodies that orbit the sun, most often **between** the orbits of Mars and Jupiter. Thousands of asteroids have already been observed, and astronomers continue to discover more.

The oval-shaped orbits of some asteroids occasionally bring these bodies quite near our planet, Earth. Certain meteorite craters **on** Earth's crust may be the result **of** bombardment **by** the Apollo asteroids. Mining sites planned for these areas may bring us more information about the craters and the celestial bodies that caused them.

Scientists have considered various theories about the origin of asteroids, and it is likely that not all asteroids were formed in the same way. Asteroids may be fragments of a planet destroyed **in** the far past, or they may be material that failed to condense **into** a single planet. Some scientists believe that **asteroids** may be matter from the nuclei of ancient comets.

Asteroids vary greatly **in** size. The largest known asteroid is Ceres, which was discovered in 1801; its diameter is about 600 miles. Other large asteroids include Juno, Pallas, and Vesta. Icarus, discovered **in** 1949, is one of the smallest known asteroids; it has a diameter of just 0.6 miles.

page 119
Writing plans will vary.

page 120
First drafts will vary.

page 121
1. It is a heroic poem because the subject is not humorous., **2.** There are two stanzas. The separate grouping of lines has space above and below it., **3.** These stanzas are quatrains. Quatrains have four lines., **4.** These two stanzas tell about a ship that is headed into a hurricane.

5. The skipper he stood beside the helm,
    His pipe was in his mouth,
And he watched how the veering flaw did blow
    The smoke now West, now South.

Then up and spake an old Sailor,
    Had sailed to the Spanish Main,
"I pray thee, put into yonder port,
    For I fear a hurricane."
6. a, b, c, b, a, b, c, b

page 122

Answers will vary. Suggested:

Clenched fist
fingers curled resolutely around pen
eyes intent on paper
boring great holes through question sheet
forcing deep impressions on desk underneath
Mind blank
glazed eyes gazing far off
dancing limbs upon hot sand kernels
cooling water lapping upon toes
escape
What is the girl in the red dress doing
looking at the same line
for an hour?

page 123

Writing plans will vary.

page 124

First drafts will vary.

page 125

1. glossary, index, **2.** table of contents, **3.** copyright page, **4.** index, **5.** index, **6.** preface, **7.** title page, copyright page, **8.** table of contents, **9.** title page, **10.** table of contents

page 126

1. pages 46–48, index, **2.** pages 27–39, table of contents, **3.** pages 35, 36–37, index, **4.** pages 53–67, table of contents, **5.** pages 93, 94, 95, 96, index, **6.** pages 76–90, table of contents

page 127

African Grasslands
 I. Plants of the grasslands
  A. Trees
  B. Grasses
  C. Herbs
 II. Animals of the grasslands
  A. Large predators
   1. Lions and other cats
   2. Hunting dogs
  B. Large grazing animals
   1. Giraffes
   2. Zebras
   3. Elephants
  C. Birds
   1. Ostriches
   2. Weaver birds
   3. Eagles

1. Stevens, Beth Dvergsten. <u>Colorful Kites</u>. Logan, IA: Perfection Learning, 2000., **2.** "Unmasking Skin." <u>National Geographic</u>, November 2002, pp. 36–63.

page 128

Sentences will vary.

page 129

1. noun, **2.** adverb, **3.** the first syllable, **4.** fortune, **5.** to add minerals or vitamins to, **6.** fortunate, **7.** five, **8.** yes, **9.** No; it includes definitions that are not related to the topic of defense. This page is most likely from a dictionary.

page 130

1. 500–599 Pure Sciences, **2.** 700–799 Arts, Recreation, **3.** 800–899 Literature, **4.** 900–999 History, Geography, **5.** 400–499 Linguistics, Language, **6.** 200–299 Religion, **7.** 600–699 Applied Sciences, **8.** 600–699 Applied Sciences, **9.** 100–199 Philosophy, **10.** 300–399 Social Sciences, **11.** 900–999 History, Geography, **12.** 000–099 General Reference Books, **13.** 900–999 History, Geography, **14.** 600–699 Pure Sciences, **15.** 400–499 Linguistics, Language

page 131

1. Look in the card catalog under *Smith, Bill* for titles of books he has written. Enter *Smith, Bill—author* in the computer., **2.** Look in the card catalog under *Forten, James—subject*. Make a list of titles. Enter *Forten, James—subject* in the computer. Make a list of titles held by your library branch., **3.** No. This would give you dozens of titles, without telling you which books covered the topics best. Enter *Boston Massacre—subject* and *Boston Tea Party—subject* in the computer to limit the number of titles., **4.** Enter *Pre-Revolutionary America—title* into the computer. **5.** subject, **6.** author, **7.** title

page 132

1. dictionary, **2.** atlas, encyclopedia, **3.** *Books in Print*, **4.** almanac, current encyclopedia, **5.** thesaurus, dictionary, **6.** encyclopedia, **7.** encyclopedia, **8.** *Books in Print*, **9.** atlas, encyclopedia, **10.** encyclopedia, almanac, **11.** almanac, **12.** thesaurus, dictionary, **13.** *Books in Print*, **14.** almanac, **15.** encyclopedia, *Books in Print*

page 133

Answers will vary.